Observing
Young
Children

Education at SAGE

SAGE is a leading international publisher of journals, books, and electronic media for academic, educational, and professional markets.

Our education publishing includes:

- accessible and comprehensive texts for aspiring education professionals and practitioners looking to further their careers through continuing professional development

- inspirational advice and guidance for the classroom

- authoritative state of the art reference from the leading authors in the field.

Find out more at: **www.sagepub.co.uk/education**

Tina Bruce | Stella Louis | Georgie McCall

Observing
Young
Children

Los Angeles | London | New Delhi
Singapore | Washington DC

Los Angeles | London | New Delhi
Singapore | Washington DC

SAGE Publications Ltd
1 Oliver's Yard
55 City Road
London EC1Y 1SP

SAGE Publications Inc.
2455 Teller Road
Thousand Oaks, California 91320

SAGE Publications India Pvt Ltd
B 1/I 1 Mohan Cooperative Industrial Area
Mathura Road
New Delhi 110 044

SAGE Publications Asia-Pacific Pte Ltd
3 Church Street
#10-04 Samsung Hub
Singapore 049483

Editor: Marianne Lagrange
Editorial assistant: Rachael Plant
Production editor: Katie Forsythe
Copyeditor: Audrey Scriven
Proofreader: Thea Watson
Marketing manager: Dilhara Attygalle
Cover design: Wendy Scott
Typeset by: C&M Digitals (P) Ltd, Chennai, India
Printed in India at Replika Press Pvt Ltd

Library of Congress Control Number: 2014935065

British Library Cataloguing in Publication data

A catalogue record for this book is available from
the British Library

MIX
Paper from
responsible sources
FSC® C016779
www.fsc.org

ISBN 978-1-4462-8580-0
ISBN 978-1-4462-8581-7 (pbk)

DEDICATIONS

We have chosen to dedicate this book to the values and ideals of **Nelson Mandela**, in his efforts towards a new South Africa, free from the atrocities and social injustice of the apartheid era. Archbishop Desmond Tutu gave a tangible image through his phrase 'the Rainbow Nation'.

There are those who do good work quietly across the years and are rarely acknowledged for the important contribution they have made to improving the quality of the lives of young children.

Nel Redelinghuys is one of these people. Her work as a teacher of young children in Johannesburg, initiating an early education group for black children during the years of apartheid and then subsequently supporting developments in Soweto, has been undertaken quietly, with sustained commitment.

We would like, in this small way, to recognise her dedicated efforts for the Rainbow Nation.

CONTENTS

ABOUT THE AUTHORS

Tina Bruce CBE is an honorary visiting professor at the University of Roehampton, having originally trained as a teacher at the Froebel Educational Institute. She was also trained at the University of Manchester to teach children with hearing impairments and taught in both special and mainstream school contexts. She was head of the Froebel Research Nursery School in the Froebel College, becoming Director of the Centre for Early Childhood Studies in what is now called the University of Roehampton. She has worked with the British Council (New Zealand and Egypt) and was awarded International Woman Scholar by the University of Virginia Commonwealth.

She has published many articles and has a long and successful track record of publishing books with Sage: these include *Exploring Learning: Young Children and Blockplay* (edited by Pat Gura with the Froebel Blockplay Research Group directed by Tina Bruce), *Developing Learning in Early Childhood* and *Essentials of Literacy* (co-authored with Jenny Spratt). She was also editor of *Early Childhood: A Student Guide* and the award winning book *Early Childhood Practice: Froebel Today*.

She is a vice-president of the British Association for Early Childhood and a trustee of the Froebel Council.

Stella Louis MA is an early years consultant who has worked as a nursery nurse, nursery manager, DCE course coordinator and Early Years Training coordinator. She wrote her first book in 2008 on understanding children's schemas and has had articles published in *Nursery World* and *Early Education*. Stella has developed a sustained interest in working with parents and is involved in research on sharing knowledge and understanding of young children's schemas with parents. Stella is currently studying for a Doctorate in Education at Roehampton University and is a Froebelian-trained travelling tutor, working in the UK and in South Africa in an initiative funded by the Froebel Trust.

Georgie McCall trained with the NNEB nursery nursing qualification and subsequently trained as a teacher at Goldsmiths College. She is an extremely experienced teacher who has been Head of Ann Bernadt Nursery School and Children's Centre for over twenty years. She has great expertise in working with children with special educational needs and developing parental involvement and outdoor play. She also has considerable experience in training early years staff in the inner city both in London and in Sierra Leone (with the VSO). She is a travelling tutor with the Froebel Trust in Soweto.

ACKNOWLEDGEMENTS

Ann Bernadt Nursery School and Children's Centre
Yerebri and Marcia

Barbados Playgroup, Hampshire
Karen Strudwick, Patricia Lobb, Hayley Barnett, Sam Wickers, Jody Barnett
and Stuart Pavey, Samantha and Derek Day, Graham Barnett

Eastwood Nursery School and Children's Centre
Jo Dabir Alwi, Nicola Fletcher, Liz Rook

God's Grace Daycare
Helen Adeleke and Alice Cezimbra Canal

Hampton Wick Infant and Nursery School Head, Heidi Johnson-Paul, Edward
Humble, and Brenda and John Spencer

Kings House School
Mark Turner, Sally Crawley, Jane O'Brien, Zoe Couch, Claire Smith, Samantha
Barlow, Michele Hughes, Jinny Harris, Stacey Barber, Felicity Nesbitt, the
Adkins family, the Mallinson family, the Harrington family

Vanessa Nursery School
Michele Barrett, Sian Thompson, Rosalyn Obanishola, Jemma Hunt, Joanna
and Nima

Sthembiso and Sabeliwe Thabethe for all their invaluable help driving us to
our work and to meet colleagues during our times in Soweto.

INTRODUCTION

At most times in history, and in most parts of the world, the first seven years are regarded as the time when children learn who they are, about those who are significant to them, and how their world is. They take part, and if sensitively helped by those around them, they contribute creatively and imaginatively. They grow and develop physically. They develop empathy, compassion and thoughtful feelings.

This is a book about the process of finding user-friendly and purposeful ways of observing and planning that will help parents and practitioners to become informed and able to help young children to develop and learn. It is designed to support those who are working with young children and their families in a variety of group settings. It is also about looking with insight at children and providing them with what they need in order to develop and learn optimally, examining the historic background of observing and planning, and describing examples of good practice in different group settings. It helps to monitor a child's progress – what is needed now and to work out what is needed next.

Children learn through and with the people they love and the people who care for them. They learn through being physically active, through real, direct experiences, and through learning how to make and use symbolic systems, such as play, language and representation. Whether children are at home, or attend group settings, they need informed adults who can help them. This book will help those who work with young children so that all the developing and learning of the earliest years can be consolidated during middle childhood, hopefully in ways that will build on what has gone before.

This book gives high status to adults (i.e. parents and early childhood specialists of all kinds) who love and work with children. Observation has a long and time-honoured history and this will be explored in the book.

Observing children in spontaneous situations in a variety of other settings, the book emulates the spirit of Susan Isaacs working in the 1930s and 40s. She used theory as a lens to interpret carefully made observations and recorded the progress of children, showing the importance of observation that indicates what is needed to support and extend children's development and learning. The book is full of examples of good practice in recording observations that can then inform planning. Unless we know, tune into and understand our children, unless we act effectively on what we know, we cannot help them very much.

Clinging to dogma ('I believe that children need ...') or saying 'What was good enough for me ...' is not good enough. Children deserve better than that. The pursuit of excellence means being informed. This book will help adults increase their knowledge and understanding of the young children they work with by using observation which will inform their planning: they can then act for the good in the light of this.

All the examples given in this book can be used with different National Framework documents worldwide. However, this cannot be done in a tightly prescribed way because the book's authors share the concerns of many parents and educators of all kinds working with young children – that curriculum frameworks must be used as a resource and never as a limiting straitjacket.

GLOSSARY

The glossary which follows contains some of the key terms used in this book. You may wish to refer to this before you read the book or while you read it, or perhaps use it as a way of pulling together some of the strands explored in the following chapters.

Anecdotal records

These are a tried and tested way of gathering observations. In a busy group setting it is not always possible or desirable to have a notepad or sticky note at the ready to jot down on-the-spot observations. Anecdotal records are compiled after the time of the observation, with quiet reflection, when alone, with a colleague or parent, or with the child, after the event has taken place. (For example, at the end of the day, or the end of the week.) They can be written, annotated photographs (often of constructions, dances, action in the sand, water, garden) or examples of paintings, drawings etc.

Because of this, it may only be possible to give a rough date and time of day when the observation was made, but it goes without saying, the more accurate the better, and it should be noted if there is guessing included. Often a practitioner or parent will say, 'Oh, I've just remembered, the other day he spent half the afternoon in the garden looking under stones! He's doing it again today. This might be significant, so I'll write it down'. Or looking through the anecdotal records the practitioner might notice that Jodie always waves goodbye to her mother, and then goes to the clay table for a focused time there. This makes it clear that this is the way she self manages the transition from Mother being there to Mother going to work. It will therefore be important to make sure there is always a clay table for her, so as not to disturb the way she deals with this so positively.

Anecdotal observations are a useful way of adding to and enhancing the other kinds of records, and are often helpful in adding detail to family scrapbooks and child profiles. But they are not as reliable or accurate as other methods if they are made too long after the event, because our memories can sometimes play tricks on us. On the other hand, they often bring alive the way a child engages, or not, with their learning. They are useful in bringing us to consider what a child is interested in and needs.

Diaries

These are dated anecdotal records, but because they are kept on a daily basis, they can become a great burden.

Formative records

These are records which build up gradually and continuously over time. They are the most useful kind of record, as they help us to see how individual children are learning, and how we are helping them to learn well. They will involve us in keeping narrative records. Formative records emphasise the process of developing and learning and help us to monitor progress.

Narrative records

There are several different kinds of narrative record, but they all aim to give the date, the time of day when an observation was made, and the duration of the observation, albeit with varying degrees of preciseness. Anecdotes are the least precise kind of narrative record compared with running records or specimen records, which are both made on the spot. Narrative records use the following methods: writing, diagrams, sketches, electronic recordings and photographs (still and moving sequences). Nowadays they are increasingly being stored on computer, with booklets printed off for parents to keep as home records and family memories of the children's learning while attending the setting. These often become treasured family possessions.

On-the-spot narrative records

1 Running records This type of narrative observation is typical in that it is made on the spot and notes what a child does and says (i.e. actions and language). The date and the starting and finishing time are recorded. Later on, the observation can be added to (using a different coloured pen, since these will be anecdotal records). Still later that day (ideally), or if not at the end of the week, running records can also be looked at with a particular focus or coded in particular ways.

2 Specimen records These narrative observations are also made on the spot. They note actions and language, as well as information about the situation and place. Again, the date and starting and finishing time are noted. Details can be filled in later (with a different colour pen, as the additions are anecdotal records).

Because specimen records give the actions, language and context in which these took place, they are able to yield rich quantities of information, which can be reflected on later that day (ideally) or later that week to take a particular focus, or to code according to particular emphases.

Planning

It is important to distinguish between plans and planning.

Plans tend to be set in concrete and therefore inflexible. They do not often take account of the educational needs of individual children. They also tend to be separate and remain unattached to anything save for what is supposed to be covered in official framework documents. 'Transmission' describes their approach. This means beginning with what the official framework document says should be covered, and then breaking this down and teaching it (transmitting it) in small manageable chunks, week by week, until everything that is required has been transmitted.

Planning is an active process which helps us to look ahead, organise, manage and review what we offer to children and their families, and to act on this. The planning process involves us in making longer-term plans (e.g. FLOW charts) and in seeing 'Possible Lines of Direction' (PLOD charts) as well as weekly and daily plans which link with the formative records we keep of each child's progress. The planning process enables us to link what we have observed as important for the child in developing his/her learning with what is required in official framework documents. Planning is the bridge which links the two.

Schemas

Schemas are a set of repeatable actions, which can be generalised in different situations. The experiences of life are integrated into these patterns and are gradually coordinated. Coordinations lead to higher-level and more powerful schemas. (Athey, 1990: 35–7)

Summative records

At regular intervals we willl need to take stock of where a child is in his/her development and learning. We will need to look at what we are offering the child and the family. Summative records can help us review what is going on at a particular time. These focus on results and products, rather than how they came about. Such records help us evaluate what we offer the child. They also help us identify children's special educational needs and disabilities.

The most useful summative records can be compiled easily from the formative records, by giving them a particular *focus*, by looking at the way they have been *coded*, by reviewing the *FLOW* or *PLOD* charts and related *planning* records. These can be used when sharing progress with parents, colleagues in the same setting, or colleagues from other agencies. Many settings now keep formative observations in electronic forms which can also be printed off as booklets for families. These days it is usually the norm that summative records are electronically stored.

Standardised tests of various kinds can be useful in confirming (or not) children's progress and in helping to pin-point (diagnose) their strengths and difficulties. However, if standardised summative tests dominate they lose their usefulness, and children are then tested rather than assessed. This in turn creates an atmosphere of fear in the children because they quickly pick up on the fact that their parents as well as staff are anxious about the results. It is not healthy when there is a sense of those external to the situation holding all the power and creating such pressure for children to achieve in narrow ways. In countries where there is a narrowing of the curriculum a situation develops where schooling is externally assessed and judged: this might interfere with children's education more than it supports it. This book is about educating young children with an emphasis on helping each child to develop and learn. Planning as a constantly flowing process (rather than making inflexible plans) is a crucial part of this.

CHAPTER 1

WHY KEEP RECORDS?

In this chapter, you will learn about:

- The difference between assessment and evaluation.
- The reasons why observation is important.

We need to keep records so that staff and parents can do their best for each child and each group of children. Through getting to know a child, we also get to know how to help that child develop in all aspects and learn more, and we can recognise what to offer the child next. Getting to know that child is about:

- **assessment** – i.e. the child's progress;
- **evaluation** – i.e. what we have offered, are offering and what, in the light of what we find, we decide we will offer the child next;
- our records – which we will need in order to **link** assessment with evaluation.

There is no 'royal road' to record-keeping. Each team in each setting will need to find its own way, including parents and children as part of the process. The record-keeping will need to feel owned by every person working with it.

Observing children in a variety of situations

As soon as words like assessment and evaluation are used, there is a tendency to think that children should be observed in testing conditions, or structured activities led by adults. It is important to observe each child in a variety of situations so as to build up a full picture of the whole child. Observing spontaneous play will help us plan. Observing children at play is a key aspect by which we may assess and develop learning for children. An assessment of the whole child becomes possible, not to mention fascinating, if a child is observed:

- in transition – e.g. arriving in the setting and changing from being with a parent/carer to being with a keyperson and other children/friends.
- leaving – e.g. probably tired.
- making choices – e.g. meandering apparently purposeless, but in fact probably assessing what is on offer, and deciding what to do, or needing help to access a group playing, etc.
- at play – e.g. alone, with another child, with an adult, and with a group of children (which includes or does not include an adult).
- during mealtimes – e.g. enjoying the food, appearing wary of it, slow to eat, enjoying the company and conversation, anxious.
- settling for a sleep, where this is needed.
- taking part in an adult-led experience – e.g. walking to buy ingredients for cooking at the shop, doing cookery, at the woodwork bench, at the graphics table, or choosing to be in the workshop area making models, negotiating the blockplay area, talking to him-/herself while playing with small world toys, with the adult supporting the development of characters inhabiting the miniature world, and the story that is emerging.

Practitioners do not have to hang back when observing and participant observation is a good way to gather observations. It is easier to hear what children say, and if the observation is immediately recorded on a stick-it label it will be as near on the spot as it can be; if anecdotal, it is easier to remember back when you have taken part in the conversation.

The influences upon us

It is almost impossible not to be influenced by the historic and cultural era in which we operate. Those of us who work with young children are – whether conscious of it or not – inextricably linked with what is happening in relation to current official policy in the country in which we live and work.

When the present influences us at an unconscious level its impact is usually powerful, as is propaganda or subliminal advertising. It is therefore important to become conscious of the influences upon us.

A good quality curriculum for young children anywhere in the world is not possible without good record-keeping. However, while it is easy to agree that quality record-keeping is 'a good thing' it is quite another to develop the required systems for doing this.

Of course, no one would want to be told what to do in relation to record-keeping. Yet it does seem from conversations with colleagues working with young children in different countries, and in a variety of settings, that people would certainly appreciate help, support, and concrete encouragement in developing their own strategies for tackling such a demanding, challenging, and difficult area.

The more early childhood practitioners – including teachers and the wide range of practitioners working with young children in settings – work with health visitors, child minders, therapists and parents, the better the progress that will be made.

We need adequate staff/child ratios

If we are to make good records, we will need sufficient space during the day to write these. We need the courage to remember that one in-depth observation is worth 30 superficial daily ones. Because young children develop in an integrated way, the same observation may yield information about several aspects of a child's progress.

Practitioners need to be trained in child observation and able to use minute observation techniques, especially the different kinds of narrative records or anecdotal records. All of this will help them create a picture – a vignette – of the whole child. They will also be able, through in-service training, to observe generalised patterns in each child's development, and then adjust what they offer that child to further his/her learning. By providing for individual children they can use records to cater for groups of children as well. (This is discussed later in the book.)

Practitioners who have been trained in observation value the need for good observation of individual children, and are concerned that they use this to inform their curriculum organisation and planning. They want to support children using traditionally successful early-years provision of materials, opportunities, experiences and relationships with others. They also want to improve their effectiveness in extending children in their learning, working as a team whilst acting as individual family workers. They see good record-keeping as central to this process. This book shows how narrative records traditionally used by early childhood workers remain the basis of record-keeping, but are gradually being put to better use, becoming less time- and energy-consuming, and more effective. This is because one observation gives a clue and the build-up of continuous observations can be used to reflect on a child's progress from various viewpoints – for example, relationships, developments in play, mathematics, language and literacy, or imagination.

Record-keeping is about getting to know each child to the best of our ability, in ways which do not cause us to burn out or give up, despite the enormity of the challenge given the present constraints upon us. Without good record-keeping we cannot work well.

Reflections on this chapter

- Do your recording of observations and your planning to support the development and learning of the children you work with encourage you to get to know each child?
- Using your records and the data you have gathered are you able to see how various groups of children are developing and learning? Do the children with English as an additional language make good progress in relation to monolingual children in your setting, for example? In other words, can you analyse your observations and use them to facilitate the education (a concept which includes care) of those children?

📖 Further reading

Dowling, M. (2013) *Young Children's Thinking*. London: Sage.

Hutchin, V. (2013) *Effective Practice in the Early Years Foundation Stage: An Essential Guide*. Maidenhead: Open University Press, in Association with Nursery World.

Whitebread, D. (2012) *Developmental Psychology and Early Childhood Education*. London: Sage.

CHAPTER 2

WHAT WORKS IN OBSERVATION AND RECORD-KEEPING?

> **In this chapter you will learn about:**
>
> - How observation has a powerful legacy to hand on to current practitioners.
> - How we can use the past to inform and develop our current observational techniques.

Lessons from the past

If we look back to the lessons that history can teach us these can prove powerful. The current debates about record-keeping are not new. They have raged in one form or another at least since the middle of the eighteenth century. They have never been resolved, and we cannot expect to resolve them completely today. However, we can try to see with clarity what the main issues have always been, and how people have tackled them. We can identify the principles which occur again and again in the keeping of good records. Having identified these, we can then translate them in terms of the settings we work in today, and thus make good records, feel ownership of them, and have confidence in them. Record-keeping is an integral part of our whole approach to working with young children and those close to them. It cannot be set apart from everything else that we do. Almost half a century ago Almy (1975: 227) stated:

> ... unless it helps teachers to capitalise on children's strength and support their weaknesses, such procedures had better be abandoned ... Records have value only to the extent that the staff puts them to use in guiding and instructing children.

There is probably considerable agreement that keeping records is 'a good thing', but as the song says 'It ain't what you do, it's the way that you do it' – and that is what this chapter is about.

Baby biographies in the eighteenth-century

We know that it is the people who love children and who are committed to them who are prepared to go to great lengths for them. It is therefore not surprising that the first examples of quality record-keeping were made by parents. Until the end of the eighteenth century the infant mortality rate was high in the first year of life, but in 1774 Johann Heinrich Pestalozzi wrote *A Father's Diary* about his three-and-a-half year old son, and in 1787 Dietrich Tiedmann wrote about his son's first three years of life. Likewise in 1877 Charles Darwin published the observations of his son Doddy (William Erasmus) based on observations made thirty-seven years before. (See Irwin and Bushnell, 1980; Navarra, 1955.)

What we can learn from the eighteenth-century baby biographies

1. Early baby biographies demonstrate how important it is to look, listen and enjoy being with children. It is only through doing this that we can really get to know a child and understand his or her development and learning.
2. Baby biographies remind us of the importance of being in a natural setting. Irwin and Bushnell (1980: 5) point out that 'each child exhibits his or her own preferred learning style if the adult will just watch for clues.'
3. Our own personal philosophy of life influences what we observe. The observations we make and the records we keep are direct products of our framework of thinking, feeling and relating to children and their families. Sylva and Moore (1984) found that records kept in tightly structured nurseries tended to use checklists, while indirectly and informally structured nurseries kept narrative-type records. In other words, the philosophy of the staff affects the record-keeping style.
4. Knowing what our philosophy is empowers our work. If we are not aware of the philosophy that influences us, our observations will be random, uninformed, and thus incapable of being used to inform our forward-planning and organisation of the curriculum. Irwin and Bushnell say (1980: 3):

   > ... once we have trained ourselves to become keen observers, we can turn our attention to becoming shrewd interpreters of what we observe. What we see, and what we think about what we see, will naturally raise questions as to what actions we might take. Identifying, recording, hypothesising, questioning, theorising, changing, these are all part of the cycle of discovery for every observer.

5. Charles Darwin moved through this whole cycle, and his records, including his baby biography of Doddy, contributed to the revolution in thinking about the origin and development of the species. We cannot separate observation from recording. We cannot record unless we observe. In order to keep good records, baby biographies from the eighteenth century teach us that we need to observe so that we can support and extend the development and learning of the child (Bruce, 1987; 1991; 2011a).
6. Parents are central to this process.

The Child Study Movement

Irwin and Bushnell (1980: 23) suggest that three men contributed to the emergence of the child study movement during a period spanning the 1870s to the 1950s. First was Charles Darwin (1809–1882), who as we have seen published his observations of his son, Doddy, in 1877. Then Granville Stanley Hall (1844–1924), who founded the *American Journal of Psychology* and organised conferences hosted at Clark University. His students included Dewey, Gessell and Terman. Irwin and Bushnell (1980: 25) suggest that Darwin's influence and Hall's enthusiasm and promotion gave rise to the burgeoning Child Study Movement. This was further promoted when Lawrence Kelso Frank (1890–1968) administered the grants of the Spelman Rockefeller Memorial in the 1920s, which brought wide dissemination.

The home-based baby biographies written by parents such as Charles Darwin gave way to child studies written by professionals trained in observation – and eager to analyse. Indeed some of the professionals (such as Navarra, 1955) studied their own children.

Published child studies have not been so widespread since the 1960s, but as we shall see below the publications making use of them are greatly valued because they give us such insight as children develop and learn. More than anything else, they show us how to provide children with what they need.

What we can learn from the Child Study Movement

1. **When parents and professional workers join together, they make a powerful and constructive partnership.** Parents have always been deeply involved in the development and learning of their children. They were amongst the first record keepers of their children's progress. The Froebel Nursery Project (1972–1977), directed by Chris Athey, demonstrated that parents are hungry for help in this area, and deeply appreciative of it. Research by Hughes et al. (1990) also echoed the fact that parents want to work closely with professionals and that they are not out to challenge. They wish to become informed together with the educators who work with their children and to share their children's progress

with them in a spirit of partnership. During the twentieth century, parents and grandparents continued to make child studies: for example, Piaget in the 1920s, Navarra in 1955, Bissex, Grübacker and Matthews in the 1980s, and Arnold in 1999 and 2003.

o   Piaget (1920s)

His early work involved observing his three children in natural settings and this is probably when he did his best work. Unfortunately he later switched to comparing test groups of children on adult-set tasks in laboratory settings. This led to a serious under-estimation of what children could achieve, since tests do not allow children to function at their highest levels (Donaldson, 1978).

o   Navarra (1955)

John Navarra and his wife observed and recorded the development of scientific concepts in their six year old son L.B. in a home situation. Two important points are made by Navarra (1955: 26): firstly, that 'all data no matter what the source, must be viewed in context against a complete pattern', however one example may serve as a clue or pointer; and secondly, that spontaneous activity yields the most useful information for record-keeping (1955: 20) – 'The study of play activity becomes the most important device by which insight was gained concerning the conceptual development of the child'. Navarra added (1955: 30) 'on the few occasions when he [L.B.] was put on the spot, superficial replies were obtained'.

The set of observations gathered in this invaluable book show L.B. gradually teasing out the difference between steam and smoke as he develops scientific concepts.

o   Ruth Weir (1970s)

Ruth Weir's study of her two year old son Anthony and his pre-sleep monologues have proved invaluable for those researching language development, as have other studies such as Paul West's *Words for a Deaf Daughter* (1972), or Glenda Bissex looking at her son Paul's early writing and reading from five-and-a-half to eleven years old (1980).

o   John Matthews (1988)

John Matthews has made a longitudinal study of the drawings, paintings and constructions of his three children (Ben, Joel and Hannah) from birth to adolescence. These have been mainly in the home setting since he was present while they were drawing, painting and constructing. His research is explored in depth in his books (2003) and his work observing chimpanzees in a zoo in Singapore has also been published (Matthews, 2011).

2. **Being clear about our philosophy means that we can look at other theories critically and with interest.** It is not the intention of this book to spend time examining in great detail the influence of behaviourist psychology theory on record-keeping from the 1920s. Suffice it to say that overall this has had the damaging impact of over-valuing unnatural settings and adult-led pre-structured tasks and introducing pre-structured record sheets. Records of children were confined to those who could or could not manage to do what the adult's task required, and a 'sheep and goats' element began to creep in. Christine Hardyman writes (1984: 165) 'Frederick Truby King and John B. Watson both came to the study of children from the study of animals, and their debts to it are all too obvious'.

Chris Athey summed up this approach (1990: 30):

> ... in programmes where the focus is on one way transmission of information, teachers find it difficult to advance their knowledge of child development because so much time is taken up with the content to be transmitted.

The transmission of information approach contrasts with the view taken in this book that sees development as the motor for learning. It emphasises the child as an active learner rather than a passive receiver of knowledge.

3. **We need to tease out the relationship between development and learning.** If we do not do this, we shall not know how we want to work with children and their families, what our records are for, or how to make use of them. We want our records to have purpose and function, to help us provide in educationally worthwhile ways across the curriculum. Otherwise our records will not be worth all the effort of writing, photographing, etc. Development is about the general situations in which children spontaneously function. It is the engine which drives children to learn. For example, Matthew, at two years old, can run and jump, but he can't yet hop or skip. He loves to run across open spaces, and to jump to music. Learning is not spontaneous. It is sparked by another person or by a situation. Learning is provoked, and limited to the particular situation, moment or specific problem to be tackled. Matthew is taken to a gymnasium and invited to run. He is taken to a country field, where running is more of a problem on a less even surface. Having developed the ability to run and jump, Matthew is learning to run in particular situations. He goes to the fair, where he learns how to jump on an inflatable castle, a specific situation with particular problems.

Most of the learning children do happens as they develop. We don't even notice that they are learning. It is one of nature's safety mechanisms. It is actually difficult to stop children learning providing they are with people who encourage their general development, that is, providing it is known that two year olds love to run and jump because developmentally that is what two year olds need to do. Children would be constrained from learning if they were not allowed to develop normally in this way, and we have seen tragic instances of this in the orphanages of Romania where children, sitting in cots all day, have developed learning difficulties partly through their development being constrained. Where general development is constrained through a disability, we also have to be imaginative in providing learning experiences. For example, blind children rarely crawl because it is frightening for them to set off into the unknown (Chapman, 1978; Nielsson, 1985, 1993).

The more adults know about general development, the more appropriately they will be able to plan and so extend children's learning. Records need to show what adults observe, and how they support and extend, using the relationship between development and learning to do so.

4. **We need to look at the implications of being trained observers and recorders of children's development and learning.** Although baby biographies in the eighteenth century meant those close to the child could savour and share the records later, this did not help adults in planning and organising the next steps in learning. It accentuated past achievements, milestones in development and growing points. Modern-day parents often keep baby albums full of labelled photographs which are treasured for precisely these reasons. These show the first smiles, teeth, sitting, crawling, walking, birthdays ...

By contrast the Child Study Movement emphasised the use, purpose and function of observation and recording. Adults were not only to observe and support children's development, they were also to extend this by helping children to learn.

5. **We need to consider how much we should pre-structure what we shall observe** – if we don't, how will we know what to record? Sinn, quoted by Navarra (1995), who made a child study in 1894, wrote of the importance of observing and recording what a child does in a natural setting, since what the child does is meaningless and trivial until it is illuminated by some other action days or weeks after; bits of the mosaic from far apart have to be fitted together before it is intelligible.

In the 1930s, Susan Isaacs also stressed that it was the child's spontaneous interests, feeling and intellectual life which were significant and worthy of recording. When we begin to pre-structure and manipulate the situation, asking children to perform certain tasks so that we can observe and record them on a prepared form, we shall miss most of the vital information we need in order to help them learn. A book which was widely read, based on the research of Bennett and Kell (1989: 31), stated that there is a

... tendency amongst teachers to limit their assessment to the products of children's work. Rarely did they attempt to ascertain the processes or strategies employed by children in coming to their finished product.

In Sweden, the words 'teaching' and 'learning' are the same. In this book we are not using the word 'teach', which implies adults transmitting, imposing, invading and dominating children's lives. We prefer to say 'helping children to learn'. This means the adult is a facilitator, catalyst and enabler, who knows when and how to support general development, but also recognises the crucial moment when children must have direct help or planned help if they are to learn something specific. Navarra (1955) puts it very well, writing about the child study he and his wife made about their son L.B.'s development in scientific concepts. There was no attempt to 'lead the child by the nose.' It should be clear also that the child was not being 'used'. He was in the best sense of the word aided and given opportunities with the full knowledge that adults were vitally interested in him. In the process, a record was made.

6. **Narrative records seem to be the most useful for early childhood educators.** Lesley Webb (1975) emphasises the dangers of deciding in advance precisely what ought to be recorded; as she says, children often do not behave or function as they ought. What we would like children to know is often different from what they really know. In fact they often know more than we think. Dorothy Butler's study, *Cushla and Her Books* (1987), took place both at home and in school. So did that of Gordon Wells in the 1980s. This study cast light on why Rosie, aged five, appeared to function poorly at school, and how the school could work to create a more enabling environment for her. Like Dorothy Butler's study of Cushla, who is a child with special needs, Gordon Wells focused on what Rosie did and said rather than on what she could not manage to do. Similarly Virginia Axeline's study, *Dibs – In Search of Self* (1964), showed what an autistic child could do rather than could not do. Narrative records keep emphasising strengths, whilst pre-structured record forms can quickly lead to a focus on weakness, failure and 'can't do.'

7. **If you want to get ahead get a theory.** John and Elisabeth Robertson made a series of films in the 1950s using observations they made of children separated from their parents. After watching the film about a child called John and his separation from his mother, few audiences could avoid weeping. The Robertsons were influenced by John Bowlby's theory of separation and loss which has since been modified and developed.

Our observations and records, whether we like it or not, will be using our own pet theories. It is best if we know what they are! This was true in the Froebel Blockplay Research Project directed by Tina Bruce from 1987 to 1990 (Gura (ed.) 1992). This project was influenced partly by the work of Chris Athey and the inter-actionist theories of Piaget, Vygotsky and Bruner, (discussed in Bruce, 1987; 2011a,b,c). It is possible to look at Harriet Johnson's classic study of children's blockplay at Bank Street College in the 1930s and interpret her records in the light of Piagetian schemas and see patterns in what children do. Similarly, the records made by Susan Isaacs in the 1930s at the Malting House School can also be interpreted in this way.

All of these records have something in common. They are narrative records, using words, diagrams, tape recordings and photography to gather on-the-spot information which can later be used, reflected on, and focused in different ways. This kind of record gives a wealth of information which helps us look backwards or be in the present and to move forwards for each child. These records have a purpose and function. They are useful to us in a variety of ways.

8. **We need to be scientific rather than pseudo-scientific when we keep records.** In a BBC *Horizon* interview (1981) Richard Feynman, the Nobel prize-winning physicist, was clear that it was premature to try and impose on education the kind of measurement and recording techniques used in advanced physics. His reasoning was that it is much more difficult to accumulate and analyse real and useful information about children developing and learning than it is to study the atom (Bruce, 1991: Chapter 7).

In the next section we shall focus on narrative records, because these are the most helpful for early childhood educators.

Narrative records

Irwin and Bushnell (1980) list these types of narrative record: diaries, anecdotes, running records and specimen records:

1. **Diaries** are kept daily and can be a burden especially with large numbers of children.
2. **Anecdotes** are more user-friendly, even though they lack the same continuity as a diary. The advantages of recording dated anecdotes is that they can be discussed after the children go home and can be a source of deep pleasure as the record-keeper recognises which important experiences children may have had through, for example, sand play. This kind of quiet reflection also helps us to ponder some of the difficulties a particular child may be having. It is not intrusive on the children, who will often become ill at ease when they see adults observing them with notepads in hand.
3. **Running records** happen on the spot, noting a particular continuous behaviour sequence of the child. Stick-it labels on a pad are often favoured, which ensure conciseness and observations can be noted without children feeling they are being watched. This gives just enough dated information, so that later on it can be filled out on the child's profile and

any photographs taken at the time can be dated and added. Aspects of particular interest can also be coded using a letter code or different-coloured highlighter pens. This sort of record reaps a wealth of useful information (Clay, 1985).

4. **Specimen records** also note on the spot what a child says and does, but they additionally record the situation or context. This gives us enough detail at the time, but again allows more to be filled in later. We can then look at that child's progress as well as what we are offering. We can assess, evaluate, and link the two – and we can plan ahead. Lesley Webb (1975) was an advocate of this kind of narrative record. (Note that in this book, we use the term 'on-the-spot narrative record' rather than 'specimen record'.)

Figure 2.1 is an example of a specimen record taken from Lesley Webb's *Making a Start on Child Study*.

Date of observation		Child's name + date of birth + actual age
Short description of situation in which observation is being made.		
Time	What is happening	Vocalisation

Figure 2.1   Specimen narrative record from *Making a Start on Child Study* (Webb, 1975)

> Recording of on-going behaviour has to be done at break-neck speed, and even then no one of us, however proficient, can record everything a child does and says as it is happening. (Webb, 1975: 46)

We need to develop our own personal codes. Lesley Webb, for example, uses:

Q clenched fist L → pincer grip

III, spread fingers → R moves to the right

She calls this a 'rapid writing code'. These raw data can then be analysed later.

This is well worth the effort and pays off, especially if particular children are the focus for observation on particular days. In this way a child can be observed in detail regularly. One specimen description can give more information about a child's development and learning than any amount of superficial sampling. Every member of staff needs to take part so that the knowledge and ideas can then be shared. Use highlighter pens of different colours, or letter/number codes.

Sampling and rating techniques

Irwin and Bushnell (1980) give three sampling strategies, which are of limited use to busy practitioners:

1. **Time sampling** means looking, say every hour, to check what is happening either with a certain child, or with an area such as the home corner, and recording on a prepared pre-structured form using a code. It quickly encourages a superficial approach, and often turns into an elaborate way of demonstrating that no one is using the home corner, or that a child is always playing outside.
2. **Event sampling**, like time sampling, uses a prepared pre-structured form. Helen Dawes (1934) looked at quarrels as they occurred. However, because the prepared form dictates what is recorded, event sampling usually leaves out much of the interesting information that could be obtained.
3. **Checklists** are of little value. Unlike specimen records which reflect after the observation has been made through a specific focus, checklists tend to create a narrow focus so that we are inclined only to look out for what is on the prepared list. Everything else is usually ignored. Using official framework documents legally enshrined in a country, such as the EYFS in England or the Curriculum for Excellence in Scotland, as checklists could be a way towards creating a very narrow approach to the curriculum, and the kind of pre-structured, adult-dominated environment that constrains learning. Perhaps we could even say that checklists have no place as a record-keeping strategy for any adult who wants to focus on a quality curriculum. They give no detail and tell us nothing of the context or how children learn. Checklists are unlike narrative records in a very important way. When we use a checklist, we decide in advance what to focus on. When we use a narrative record we do not. We decide afterwards how to focus. We use the observation to inform the planning. We could look at the same observation with a mathematical focus, or to see how easily a child is relating to other children, or to look at a child's play.

Checklists narrow and constrain our focus, and miss out more information than they include. They give us more work. Ploughing through lists for every separate thing is a burden, and not much fun. Narrative records help us to be flexible and active in ways which bring deep learning for the child, family, and ourselves. (See the Narrative Records chart on p.15.)

Comparison between Narrative Records and Checklists

NARRATIVE RECORDS

(1) Record:

- date and time;
- what the child does;
- what the child says;
- the situation and context.

Do this on the spot.

You could use stick-it labels. Insert observations in the child's file later in the day.

(2) Fill in the detail later on (i.e. make anecdotal records, remembering extra details after the event).

Make it clear which observations are on-the-spot and which were added later (record dates).

(3) Reflect on the observations with a particular focus e.g. mathematics, language, aggression towards other children.

(4) Each observation contains a wealth of information, and it is an efficient use of your time and energy to use one or two observations in several ways, with a different focus or emphasis on each occasion.

CHECKLISTS

(1) Decide in advance what the focus of the observations will be, e.g. children's questions, science.

Make a list, or a coded list on a prepared form. Observe the child using the code or list and tick what you see.

Ignore everything that cannot be coded or ticked.

(2) A checklist will only give you limited and narrow information, which will be difficult to act on later in a deep and sensitive way.

(3) Checklists do not give the information we most need about children learning.

(4) Checklists appear to be a quick, easy way of record-keeping, but shortcuts affect our ability of offer a quality curriculum. They are not an effective use of our time and energy because they yield little information but demand intense effort which cuts into our interactions with children.

Rating scales

Rating scales tell us nothing about the causes or context and are time-consuming. They give us little information to use for forward planning. Millie Almy (1975) says 'Tests given in the early childhood years are not very good predictors of the child's later status'. The Bullock Report (DES, 1974) reminded us that you do not make children grow by measuring them.

However, practitioners have found it useful to apply rating scales such as ECERS to evaluate what they offer children in terms of, for example, physical environment and the qualifications and experience of staff working with them, infection rates in babies, or partnership with parents.

Records need both to assess the child and evaluate the curriculum we offer in ways that link

We have seen that the first records were made by parents. They focused on the child rather than on what the child was offered or would benefit from. In modern life, we still need records which assess children's progress but we also need records which help us to evaluate the curriculum we provide. It is always best to build on our strengths. Early attempts at evaluating the curriculum tended to make use of prepared charts which adults filled in to see which areas of provision children spontaneously used most frequently, regularly or rarely. This was in the spirit of the bedrock principles of the early childhood traditions (Bruce, 1987) and did not attempt to cut across the child's autonomy in learning. It is the intention of this book to keep a steady course of continuity with progression within these traditions which are summarised at the end of this chapter.

Early childhood workers are finding ways of recording their evaluations of the curriculum offered to the young children they work with in ways which hold true to time-honoured early childhood practice, informed by current theory and research. It is possible to keep faith with the traditional heritage while fulfilling legal requirements, using the heritage as a navigational tool. The remaining chapters in this book show how this is being achieved in a range of settings.

Through re-exploring early childhood work and what it stands for, as well as re-stating what is important in modern terms, we reaffirm our work and move forward.

Record-keeping needs to link assessment and evaluation

Linking our records assessing the child's progress with records evaluating what we offer children is the challenge for record-keeping as we approach the twenty-first century. Student teachers and nursery practitioners on placements have always faced this challenge in the keeping of their placement files. Keeping useful records is probably the most difficult part of working with children, and yet unless we do this we cannot do our best for children and their families. As we saw in Chapter 1, having established why we want to keep records at all, we need to find ways of doing so which do not wear us out. Burn-out is a real issue. Record-keeping should not be a burden: it should be a process which throws light on each child's learning and helps us to look at how particular groups of children are experiencing what is offered. For example, how are the boys doing? How many children are enjoying what is offered in the garden, or at the art area? What is the experience of children with English as an additional language? How inclusive is the setting for children with special educational needs or disabilities? Do parents have positive experiences?

We need a better cross-linking and getting-together of records about individual children with the notes we keep on organisation, planning and provision. What we offer needs to impinge on and relate to how the children react and initiate, or do not. For Tim, aged seven, in a class doing a project on the Romans, the project had no impact. It passed him by. He stolidly continued his interest, which was then the properties of clay, and how birds fly and eat. He was supposed to make 'Roman' pots at school, but he made meticulous clay models of a blackbird, robin, blue tit and woodpecker. The only link with the Romans was the clay. Just as the Romans passed Tim by, so his strengths passed his teacher by. She saw him as a reluctant and poor reader and writer, with a dislike of drawing and an inability to stay on task. By keeping to a pre-structured project (doing the Romans) she was kept from appreciating his deep knowledge of nature, or his advanced ability to make meticulous and exquisite three-dimensional models. She needed a record-keeping system which linked her plans and the Roman project to her individual notes on Tim.

Summary

- Early records stress assessment. Early parent/baby biographies, and the Child Study Movement, encouraged professionals to write down their observations of children's progress.
- We need a parent/professional partnership in the observation of children's progress in order to keep useful records.
- Narrative records are the most informative and efficient use of our time and energy.
- We need to keep records which assess each child and evaluate what we offer those children in ways which link with each other.
- Looking at how people in the past have approached record-keeping avoids our re-inventing the wheel.
- Our records need to build on the bedrock principles which stem from the early childhood traditions (Bruce, 1987; 2012):

  o Childhood is seen as valid in itself, as part of life and not simply as a preparation for adulthood. Thus education is seen similarly as something of the present and not just as the preparation and training for later on.
  o The whole child is considered to be important. Health, both physical and mental, is emphasised, as well as the importance of feelings, thoughts and spiritual aspects.

- Learning is not compartmentalised because everything links together.
- Intrinsic motivation – resulting in child-initiated, self-directed activity – is valued.
- Self-discipline is emphasised. (This point and the point above relate to children's autonomy.)
- There are specially receptive periods of learning at various stages of development.
- What children can do (rather than what they cannot do) is the starting point in their education.
- There is an inner structure in a child which includes the imagination, and which can be encouraged by favourable conditions.
- The people (both adults and children) with whom the child interacts are of central importance.
- Each child's education is seen as an interaction between that child and the environment he or she is in, including in particular other people and knowledge itself.

The last principle can be expressed as a triangle involving three aspects of the curriculum – the child, the context, and the content. This is shown in Figure 2.2.

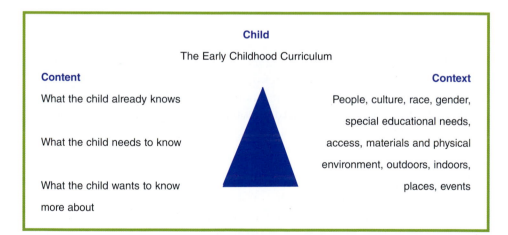

Child

The Early Childhood Curriculum

Content

What the child already knows

What the child needs to know

What the child wants to know more about

Context

People, culture, race, gender, special educational needs, access, materials and physical environment, outdoors, indoors, places, events

Figure 2.2   The three Cs of the early childhood curriculum (original source: Bruce, 1987)

Making appropriately flexible long-term plans

Record-keeping needs to be a continuing dialogue between long-term plans and the individual child's development and learning day by day and week by week. Incidental and spontaneous learning events can then be incorporated into long-term plans. This enriches the original plan.

Chris Athey (1990: 30) stated:

> ... unreflective child centredness has led to the false belief that every child requires a unique educational programme. Constructivist teachers know that many children share similar cognitive concerns.

By using long-term planning charts which are of a flexible, organic and growing nature, plans can be carried through in ways that suit children. Individuals can be catered for and particular areas of knowledge introduced. Assessment and evaluation need to be interwoven.

Can we overdo the writing down of evaluation?

Practitioners need to be aware of the possibility that we might overdo the writing down of a child's development and learning through rigidly pre-structuring our observations in ways which in the end give us less information. The same problem can apply where evaluation is concerned. There are dangers attached to writing down in advance too much about material provision, or in planning too far ahead. Practitioners need to beware of pre-structured programmes through which children are determinedly taken.

Final thoughts on current practice

This quotation from the Blockplay Research Group's publication, *Exploring Learning: Young Children and Blockplay* (edited by Gura, 1992, directed by Tina Bruce), through which five groups of staff working in five very different educational settings regularly met and discussed record-keeping in relation to blockplay, perhaps best sums up the aspirations of this chapter.

> Perhaps our most significant contribution to the record-keeping debate is the glimpses offered of the potential of record-keeping as a shared point of entry for adults and children in the gaining of insight to our own thought processes. As we develop our capacity for self-conscious thought, record-keeping becomes less formidable. (1992: 152)

What we have learned

- In this chapter we have looked at examples of current practice in record-keeping, soundly based on the principles of early childhood education. They involve parents, teamwork, observation of children and reflecting with a focus, leading to flexible advance planning.

(Continued)

(Continued)

- The ideal characteristics of useful records are:

  - They keep faith with the heritage and basic principles of the early childhood traditions.
  - They help the partnership with parents.
  - They encourage children to reflect on their own learning.
  - They are user-friendly, and make efficient, effective use of time and energy, in order that they are easy to share with parents and colleagues in the team, across disciplines (e.g. health, social services and the voluntary sector, as well as education) and with the child's future teachers.
  - They might use a variety of techniques, written, audio and video recordings, photography, files of children's work, and records of achievement.
  - They link an assessment of a child's progress with an evaluation of what that child has been offered.
  - They inform through sharing, planning and organisation, showing the progress made and the next steps both of individual children and groups of children.
  - They link with the current requirements of the day, as appropriate or legally required.
  - They are flexible.
  - They are capable of a fine focus and to yield specific information.
  - They are easy to review and summarise.
  - They show starting points as well as growth points.

Reflections on this chapter

- Which of the 12 points above are in place in your setting?
- When you read through the remaining chapters of this book, which of the ideal characteristics of good observation and informed planning via effective and meaningful records will you wish to focus on in order to take forward your thinking and practice?

Further reading

Athey, C. (1990) *Extending Thought in Young Children: A Parent Teacher Partnership.* London: Paul Chapman.

Bruce, T. (2011) *Early Childhood Education* (4th edn). London: Hodder Education.

Bruce, T. (ed.) (2012) *Early Childhood Practice: Froebel Today.* London: Sage.

Bruce, T. and Spratt, J. (2011) *Essentials of Literacy from 0–7: A Whole-Child Approach to Communication, Language and Literacy* (2nd edn). London: Sage.

CHAPTER 3

WORKING TOGETHER

In this chapter you will learn about:

- The importance of getting to know each child and their family.
- How to work as a team, which includes the keyperson, inter-professional practitioners, the parents/carers and the child.
- Working in partnership to gather significant markers through observation of a child's learning journey.

Details of the setting

Vanessa Nursery School is in London. It was founded by Vanessa Redgrave, who emphasises the importance of swimming in the curriculum of babies and young children. The school has a swimming pool as an integral part of this ethos, which means children attend swimming each week. The pool is also used by other local schools.

The school is outstanding, according to Ofsted and by local reputation, and has recently developed a children's centre dimension in a building over the road, so that staff work closely with health visitors and social workers, family workers and others. This means the reach of Vanessa is greater, and families with babies and toddlers are supported as well as those families with children attending the nursery school. There is also an attractive playroom and garden which are well used.

There is a healthy eating project, which culminated in an attractive recipe book with contributions from a wide range of families suggesting low cost and simple to make nutritious meals from all over the world. There is a gardening project as well, and the school has an allotment and area in the garden for growing vegetables.

Vanessa is well known for its inclusion of children with disabilities and special educational needs, and has a wide mix of families. It is a popular school, and parents appreciate the way staff work with their children as well as the beautiful physical environment.

In this chapter we will look at the way that two families are working in partnership with the staff at Vanessa and how parent partnership is a vital part of the work there.

Vanessa Nursery School and the Early Years Foundation Stage (EYFS)

Following the introduction of the Early Years Foundation Stage (EYFS) (2012), the English Statutory Framework for children 0–5 the school takes an observe, assess and plan approach (OAP) (Bruce, 1987: 132). Observation-based assessment is built on the pioneering work of Susan Isaacs in the 1930s at the Malting House School.

The EYFS has identified seven areas of learning. These have been divided into three prime and four specific areas of learning. The prime areas are:

- personal, social and emotional development;
- physical development;
- communication and language.

The specific areas are:

- literacy;
- mathematics;
- understanding the world;
- expressive arts and design.

The first step in understanding children is to observe them in action. Observing children is a skill that must be learnt if practitioners are to support what children already know. The point that we are making here is that practitioners need to understand that learning for children is not separated into disparate areas of learning, rather that everything they do links together. The areas of learning identified in the EYFS are designed to help adults take responsibility for creating and providing a stimulating, developmentally appropriate and active learning environment for children. The EYFS (2012: 6) guidance further states that:

Each area of learning and development must be implemented through planned, purposeful play and through a mix of adult-led and child-initiated activity.

This does not however mean that adult-led activities should dominate children's play. Bruce (1997) brings the delicate boundaries between adult-led and child-initiated play to the fore. She presents it as 'a rich vein of research on play', warning that this must not become a device for children to be 'moulded into the shape adults and cultures desire, by using mechanisms such as "guided play" or "structured play"'. She acknowledges that mastering the correct balance, when adults and children are playing together, is quite a delicate exercise.

At Vanessa Nursery School staff are guided by the EYFS developmental descriptors outlined in 'Development Matters'. They use this as an initial baseline assessment when a child starts and plot this against the broad phases of development (linked to the child's actual age). They then use their observations of the child to describe development and how it progresses in context to the child's real and first-hand experiences.

Nutbrown (2011) emphasises the importance of adults making detailed and sensitive observations to really 'see' what children are doing, to make sense of their actions, recognise their achievements and to create further learning opportunities.

At Vanessa Nursery School observations that are carried out within the EYFS are purposeful. Whilst many of the observations in this chapter were spontaneous, others had been planned; both however remain important. On the one hand, spontaneous observations help the staff to capture the process of play (how a child is learning) and build up a holistic picture of the child's development and learning based on his or her understanding. These observations often show the characteristics of effective learning. On the other hand, planned observations are a useful way for staff to find out about how children are responding and interacting in the nursery environment. They also ensure that every child is observed in a focused way. The staff at Vanessa Nursery School complete six planned formative observations for each child, at a rate of two per term. However, there is no set limit regarding the amount of spontaneous observations. The key point here is that all observations must have a purpose, and are evaluated and used to inform how staff must carefully structure the learning environment.

The Tracker

The Tracker (see the Spencer Tracker in Chapter 8) enables staff to see how groups and cohorts of children are making progress. Examples here would include summer-born children, children with English as an additional language, those with special educational needs, the progress of a group in mathematics, etc.

A record should be a living document as well as continuous, and utilised when appropriate.

Observations can include: samples of children's drawings, scribbles and paintings; dated photographs; tape recordings of language and communication;

video recordings: a special book/diary between home and school. These will enable children to participate in their own record-keeping and involve parents in open recording.

Adam, his parents, and his keyperson Rosalyn

Talking with Adam's mother Nima it becomes evident that she has developed a mutually respectful and trusting relationship with Adam's keyperson. She describes how there is a genuine two-way flow of information between home and Vanessa Nursery School. This is an essential element of parent partnership. Without it, the partnership will not work. Adam is the youngest by far of her children at four years old, and his first language is Somali. Her oldest son is about to go to university. Adam is the fourth child and the youngest by thirteen years. Nima compares the experiences she had of her older children's education with that of Adam. She likes being able to discuss his progress with Rosalyn, his keyperson. She also prefers the nursery school environment to the primary school nursery attended by her older children. This is for several reasons:

- The children in the nursery school are all one size, so there are no older children who are bigger. She sees this as a great advantage for the nursery school.
- She likes the building being 'not too big'. It has a spacious feeling, with its open plan, but she does not find it overwhelming.
- She likes the keyperson system because she can talk easily to Rosalyn, and she values the daily feedback at greetings and partings.
- She values it being part of the session that parents come into the room to collect their children, rather than waiting outside with the children being sent out to parents and carers as is the case in many other schools.
- She is eager for guidance in how to help Adam's play to develop so that he gets the most out of his childhood.
- Having had three older children she is relaxed about not rushing him into early formal work. The older children have done well at school, and so she understands that play helps children to learn.
- More than anything, she makes a priority her desire that Adam will receive care and support for his learning in Vanessa Nursery School, and appreciates that she finds these.

Adam was breast fed until he was two years and eight months old. She recalls how hard he found this in the beginning. She wanted to stop before he began at the nursery school, and this went according to her plan. She is an experienced mother. He wanted to wear a hat when she stopped the breastfeeding, and this was also the case in his early days at school. However, while he settled within a week he still chose to wear the hat. This gave him a sense of security at a time of transition.

It was around the time that Adam started at Vanessa that Nima became aware of his need to wear a hat (both indoors and outdoors) which she believes gave him a sense of comfort. Nima points out that it did not have to be the same hat, he just needed a hat to help him get through this transitional period. Adam's need to enclose his head was important for him and his emotional well-being. He has an enveloping and enclosing schema. Rosalyn would observe Adam across a range of contexts. She noticed that he would remove his hat during periods of deep concentration but place it nearby. Being aware of his need to wear a hat meant that Rosalyn was able to support Adam at Vanessa, thus strengthening the links between home and the setting. Today Adam no longer needs the hat as an 'object of transition' (Bruce, 2011a). He has formed a close connection with Rosalyn and he talks a lot about her at home.

Nevertheless, his mother found it hard to be separated from him while he was at the nursery school, although initially she was disappointed that it was not possible to have a full-time place for him, but she has since found that

Figure 3.1   Adam's drawings from a morning at home with his mother

he enjoys the mornings at home with her. She is a full-time mother. She does not have to rush to get him to school on time; they can take things at a leisurely pace together, enjoying each other's company. They spend time talking about what they are sharing together. Adam loves to build with construction equipment, and also to draw.

One day, at home, Adam drew a whale 'with holes in my back. It's healing up now so that I can breathe' (Figure 3.1). This demonstrated his emerging understanding of how whales breathe while living in the sea, but as mammals needing air.

Talk and play

In the 1990s a watershed curriculum framework document, 'Starting with Quality' (DES, 1990), stated that the two most important things in educating children from birth to 5 years were *talk and play*. Research since then has heavily supported this.

Talk requires babies, toddlers and young children to spend time communicating with other children and, very importantly, with adults who are talking with (not at) them. This gives children a basis for literacy, sharing books, sharing experiences such as nature, mathematics when shopping, preparing food together, and a wealth of other quality-filled experiences. Play gives children the sensory experiences they need and which allow freedom of movement, but it also lays the foundation for the most unique thing about being a human. It opens up the world of abstract thinking, beyond the here and now. It allows children to problem solve, relate to others, pretend, imagine and create. In this way, play is the foundation of later creative arts, sciences and humanities.

The staff at Vanessa arrange workshops for parents each term, and the theme for a term might be 'Reading' or 'Writing' in the autumn and spring, and 'Mathematics' in the summer. These take place during school time, so that parents have childcare, or in the evening so that working parents can attend. The theme is linked to events organised in the school, such as 'Book Week' when parents are introduced to Book Trust packs. The chosen themes also link to staff training.

The workshops with parents given by the Deputy Head Teacher, Sian Thompson, are valued by parents. Adam's mother, Nima, is then able to have a deeper discussion with Rosalyn, his keyperson, when they meet for a regular 'parent conference' and share the records which demonstrate Adam's learning and progress.

Observations

At Vanessa Nursery School child-initiated (spontaneous) play is valued and regularly observed in planned and spontaneous observations. These types of observations are important as they reveal how children begin to make choices and decisions about what, how and where they are going to concentrate on their interests.

Adam enjoying looking at books   Sept–Oct 2013

Adam listened to the 'Owl Babies' story in key group time. He held one of the props and repeated the key phrases on cue. 'I want my mummy' said Adam in a little high-pitched voice to represent the baby owl (Bill). He listened attentively and waited for his cue to say the key phrase. When the story had finished Adam asked, 'What do owls eat?' Rosalyn offered to help Adam find out the answer to his question from the information book about owls and by looking at the content page. 'They eat mice and little birds'. ' I have mice in my home', said Adam.

Adam joins the children in his key group listening to the story. 'Wow! Said the Owl'. Rosalyn briefly talks about other stories which feature owls. Adam had taken it home to read previously. Adam listened to the story while looking closely at the pictures. 'I like owls', said Adam. He continued to listen to the story. 'The owl's eyes are open'. Adam had noticed the way the illustrator had drawn the eyes to represent closed and open. At the end of the story Adam said, 'Look at that rainbow, all those colours'.

Adam was observed sitting with Matthew looking at the information books about life cycles of different animals. 'This shark is a monster and sharks eat people and that's why I don't like them'. 'And he got ugly teeth, hee, hee', said Matthew. 'That's the mermaids, so you like them?' Matthew looks closely at the photos. 'Now I'm reading the bee one. Bees sting people and they give it to humans'. 'Now, I'm going to read about frogs'. He looks closely at the photo. 'This is the rock frog', said Adam describing the frog sitting on the rock. 'This is the friend frog', describing the photo of the two frogs mating. 'But his lip is weird'. Adam tries to illustrate what he means by stretching out his own tongue for Rosalyn to see.

Analysis:

Adam enjoys looking at a range of books and when listening to stories. He handles books with care, turning pages one at a time. He demonstrates reading-type behaviour and re-visits books that he is particularly interested in. He makes comments, which are relevant to the story, pointing out features of interest, or asks questions which relate to the book or the key characters. Rosalyn helps Adam make links to other stories featuring owls. Adam demonstrates his interest in what has been read to him and makes the distinction between real and imaginary events in stories. He is aware that information relating to facts about owls can be found in non-fiction books and using the content page, where he can quickly find answers to your questions. He uses language with a degree of sophistication and remembers and talks about things that he has some interest in or knowledge about. Adam is confident and able to talk about things that he has observed in the books that he has read or as a result of significant events in his own life. Mum said that Adam has been to the aquarium. Adam likes to be amongst other children, sharing his interest with them or responding with interest to the comments made by his peers.

Figure 3.2   Observation Sheet: Adam enjoying looking at books

Adam joining in with others' play   25.04.2013

Adam joined Bertie in the block area in the garden. They were moving the blocks around and positioning them in the available space, while deciding what to build. They decided to build a submarine. They worked together to carry the big hollow blocks and place them together horizontally to make the platform floor of the submarine. They then placed a hollow block vertically on top of the platform. They arranged particular blocks and positioned them vertically to make the side of the submarine. Adam invited other children to come and sit in his submarine and they decide where they wanted to go.

'Let's go to Toys R Us'   26.04.2013

Adam and Denario are playing together in the garden. They are sitting on the wooden trucks. 'Where shall we go?' 'Let's go to Toys R Us'. They joined their trucks together and decided who should drive. Anna suggested that to make it fair, one of them could drive the truck there and the other person could drive the truck back. They talked about how they were going to connect their trucks together.

Adam, Malik and Denario   26.04.2013

Adam engaged in play with Malik and Denario. They were playing on the slide, pretending there was water at the bottom. Each child took it in turns to go down the slide and the other two would try to save their friend.

Analysis:

Adam is now very interested in other children and is now beginning to build friendships with other children who share similar interests to him. He continues to enjoy exploring the indoor and outdoor space, developing his own ideas and trying them out, playing with what they know. Adam is now confident in his ability to approach other children and join in with their imaginary play. They use available resources to create props to support their role-play and view the project as a joint effort. The children demonstrate their mathematical ability and awareness of shape, space, size and tessellation when joining the large hollow blocks together in the horizontal position. They included features like seating and an area for steering (they may have had previous experience of submarines). On completion, he invited other children to sit in the submarine. Adam is a confident social communicator and clearly understands the need for negotiation. He demonstrates this when using words such as 'Where shall we go?' and 'let's go'. Adam demonstrates friendly behaviour and understands the rules of being together such as waiting for your turn.

Figure 3.3   Observation Sheet: Adam joining in with others

Adam's first swimming experience   Sept' 2013

Nima, Adam's mum, came to the pool area and helped Adam undress, put on his trunks and his hat. 'I want to wear the goggles', said Adam. He then asked his mum to stay but allowed her to leave, saying goodbye. Adam followed the pool routine with the support of the pool helper. He walked down the steps and said, 'I want to jump into the water'. As he became more relaxed and confident, he asked if he could go to the deep end. Adam followed the other children, adapting their movements in the water. Adam initially started to walk on his tiptoes, but for good balance Rosalyn encouraged Adam to use the whole of his foot. He explored different ways of moving in the water such as jumping, bouncing from a-b along the width of the pool. 'I can do this in my bath, you know'. He started to splash, wave his arms and move from side to side. Adam chose resources from the poolside independently, sometimes reaching for them while in the water and at other times leaving the pool to collect them. Adam at one point lost his footing but very quickly regained his balance. 'I have to be careful in the water and stay here'. Rosalyn encouraged Adam to bend his knees a little, keeping his arms out wide to help him maintain good balance. Adam moved around the pool with a little more caution. At the end of the session he told Michele and Matthew how he observed Matthew swimming. Adam placed his arms out wide and moved with big strides around the room and started to laugh.

Analysis:

Adam is now willing to explore this new environment with the support of the familiar adults and his mum. He is clearly aware that there is a pool routine and dress code that he needs to follow. He used the pool experience, which was another opportunity to explore moving freely with pleasure but this time adapting his movements to the water. Adam makes links with his home experience of moving around in the bath and shares this with his key person. Adam is active and creative in his movements and uses his upper body as well as his lower body with skill and confidence. He was not deterred when taking risks to further challenge himself and lost his footing. Adam was able to transfer his body weight to regain his balance and keep moving in the water. He was able to choose resources independently to follow his own interest and explore some scientific concepts such as floating and sinking. Adam was keen to share his observation and new experience with other adults.

Figure 3.4   Observation Sheet: Adam's first swimming experience

Figure 3.5   Emergent writing, A for Adam. Core and radial drawings

Figure 3.6   Adam's Mr Bean drawing

Adam settled easily into Vanessa Nursery School, making friends easily.

He has a very close relationship with Rosalyn, his keyperson, and talks about her at home: he wonders what she is doing at weekends, for example. He was hesitant about going into the swimming pool, but Rosalyn and Nima worked together to encourage him, suggesting that he would like to do the same as his friends, who enjoyed it.

It is interesting that when Adam is at Vanessa in the afternoons, he often chooses to do a variety of things rather than draw. When he does sometimes decide to do so his drawings are often of animals. He plans what he will draw before committing this to paper, talking as he goes. He draws lions and sharks.

Washing the windows   30.04.2013

Adam joined two other children in the garden. They were using a squidgy and rollers to wash the large pool windows. Adam soaked his roller in the bucket of water, and then pushed the roller all the way up. 'Up', he said and stood on his tiptoes to gain maximum movement. Adam used his right hand to use the tool and stayed for ten minutes, sharing the buckets of water with others.

Drawing pictures   22.05.2013

Adam along with the other children in his key group were asked if they could draw pictures or writing. Adam chose a large marker pen and drew big round shapes on his paper and then lots of lines coming out of the round shapes. Denario sat next to Adam. 'Look at my drawing. Do you know what it is? It looks like a spider'. 'Look at my picture', said Denario. 'It is for my mummy'.

Mr Bean   07.06.2013

Adam picked out the clipboard and kneeled down on the floor by the blocks to draw his own picture. Denario had decided to draw a representation of his build. 'I want to draw, too', said Adam. He gripped the pencil with his right-hand and drew a picture of a person. When he had finished he said that it was Mr Bean.

Making a Ben 10 watch   11.06.2013

Adam approached Youcef, while he was making a prop at the workshop area. 'What are you making?' Youcef made a Ben 10 watch. 'I want to make one too'. Youcef showed Adam how to make the watch. Adam drew around the cup with the pen and cut the circle out, using the scissors and being careful not to cut over the markings. Youcef gave Adam a strip of black card for the wristband and helped him attach the ends together around his wrist and attach the watch face onto the band.

Analysis:

Adam uses the tools in pretend play, in the garden area. He uses gross motor movement, making up and down and large circular movements with his right hand. He spent ten minutes focused on this play, while demonstrating his understanding that some resources have to be shared. He engages in large arm movement when drawing with large paper and marker pens on the floor. He shows evidence of the core and radial schema when drawing spiders and gives meaning to his drawings. He uses a range of tools safely with control in the workshop area and tools in the sandpit area for smoothing out pretend cement, while building the wall. Adam wants to be part of other children's play and is confident in joining in.

Figure 3.7   Observation Sheet: Adam washing the windows

Adam moving freely with confidence   Oct' 2013

Adam joined the other children at key group time. The children were exploring how their bodies could move in different ways. Adam: 'I want to move like a shark'. He lay down on his stomach and raised his feet and his arms up. He moved forward on his stomach and flapped his arms and feet. Adam was able to push himself forward. 'Shark eating ducks'. The other children watched and some copied his movements and actions. 'I went to the Aquarium, you know and I saw sharks swimming'.

Adam was observed on the top garden playing with Nadine and Yasseen. 'I'm the dog', said Adam. He adjusted his body and positioned himself like a dog on the hill. He moved around with his feet and hands flat on the ground and his bottom in the air, pretending to be a dog. 'Woof, woof, woof', he said as he followed the other children over the hill.
Adam was observed attempting to travel across the monkey bars. He accepted the offer of the cones to help him to balance. Adam raised his arms and held onto on the rung and tried to place his foot onto the cones to help him balance. He tried to look forward and balance his feet on the cones at the same time. Adam was unable to hold on and lost his footing. He went back round to start again. Rosalyn said to Adam that he could co-ordinate his movements more if he placed one hand on the rung and one foot on the cone and then the other hand on the next rung and the other foot on the next cone. Adam was able to cautiously travel across the monkey bars to reach the other side.

Analysis:

Adam demonstrates his ability to co-ordinate his body to move creatively with confidence to travel in different ways. He communicates his intentions clearly to the adult and makes links with the movements and sounds that he has observed in different animals. He expresses his interest in animals when engaging in self-initiated play experiences or as a result of significant trips outside of nursery. Adam revealed that he was very interested in the feeding habits and movements of the shark. Adam likes to initiate some of his ideas and give cues for others to join in with his play. Adam demonstrates his abilty to persevere and persist and not be put off by doing things that may appear really challenging at first. He readily accepted the advice given to him by the familiar adult and was able to travel across the monkey bars with increasing confidence and revisits this skill regularly. He continues to demonstrate a strong exploratory impulse when moving in and around the garden environment.

Figure 3.8   Observation Sheet: Adam moving freely with confidence

Observations also reveal that Adam engages in pretend play. Just as the focus in his drawings is often concerned with animals, the same is true of his pretend play, when he pretends to be a dog.

Adult-led activities

Adult-led activities are based on staff observations of children's interests. At Vanessa adult-led activities can be initiated by an adult or by the children, particularly when they encounter problems in their play. The adult role is to scaffold children's learning. This means that adults must know what children need to know. In the Observation Sheets throughout this chapter (including Adam looking at a book (Figure 3.2), moving freely with confidence (Figure 3.3) and his first swimming pool experience (Figure 3.4)), Rosalyn leads his learning by making a direct contribution to what he is doing. We can see from these observations that Rosalyn not only shares a focus with Adam but that she also effectively responds to his questions and is helping him to make connections, as well as sustaining his thinking, ability and interests. To be able to tune in to him and extend his learning in this way she must know how best to support what Adam already knows. This information can only come from sensitive observations of him, rather than an over-reliance solely on the developmental descriptors outlined in 'Development Matters' (EYFS: England).

Writing up spontaneous observations

Observations of Adam included in this chapter capture the important and significant details of what he is doing.

Rosalyn's (Figure 3.3) written observation of Adam joining in others' play describes the positions and direction that the blocks are being placed in. Her description gives us key information about his ability to create enclosures of different sizes and insight into his cognitive understanding of knowing which direction to turn the blocks. In the brief observation she described what he intended to build and how he used his structure as a prop in his play to act out an event. It is clear from her observations that Rosalyn knows what to include and the right level of detail. This can only come from her being skilled and experienced in doing observations. She clearly knows about the sequences in the development of blockplay and understands the significance of what he sees. It is clear that there is a reason behind each observation no matter how brief. The important point here is that Rosalyn is capturing information about Adam that is informing her understanding about his fascinations and interests. The OAP cycle described earlier in the chapter can be seen here as Rosalyn can now use this information to inform how she provides Adam with support to extend what he already knows.

Spontaneous observations are useful for making on-going, meaningful observations of children and informing our understanding of them. These observations clearly show that Adam has an interest in journeys, which may have been missed if these are seen in isolation of the context. In the second observation in Figure 3.3, 'Let's go to Toys R Us', Rosalyn describes how the negotiation process happens. That was important. In the third written observation of Adam, Malik and Denario she describes how the boys play together doing the same thing. Each observation tells us something different about Adam. At Vanessa both planned and spontaneous observations are evaluated so that staff can plan the learning environment to enhance play. Clearly, the view of play that is held by an adult, relates to how it is interpreted and defined, and to how children are guided to express themselves. The process of evaluation supports the staff at Vanessa to critically evaluate how well the learning environment is supporting individual or groups of children.

Assessment for Learning Record

It is essential to link the observations made with the legally framed requirements of the country in which a child is being educated. It is also important that parents have a clear indication of how their children are developing.

The form below (Figure 3.9) shows the Assessment for Learning Record which is linked to the Characteristics of Learning, such as Playing and Exploring, Active Learning, and Creating and Thinking Critically.

The third page shows the age bands and where Adam's play and exploring are located.

Rosalyn uses her analysis of Adam's learning to inform his Assessment for Learning Record (AFL). These are updated twice a term. All of Rosalyn's meaningful observations of Adam help her to form an accurate picture of both his learning and future learning. It is important to reiterate that *Birth to Three Matters* (DfES, 2002) and *Curriculum Guidance for the Foundation Stage* (DfEE/QCA, 2000) are still very useful documents in helping us understand child development. It is clear that Rosalyn is both knowledgeable and confident, particularly since her initial focus remains on Adam's social competence, emotional understanding and motivation. She completed these assessments in the first term. They capture Adam's relationships, language, and his interaction with others at Vanessa Nursery School.

Characteristics of Learning

Characteristic	Observing how a child is learning	Comments
Playing and Exploring *engagement*	**Finding out and exploring** Showing curiosity about objects, events and people. Using senses to explore the world around them. Engaging in open-ended activity. Showing particular interests. **Playing with what they know** Pretending objects are things from their experience. Representing their experiences in play. Taking on a role in their play. Acting out experiences with other people. **Being willing to 'have a go'** Initiating activities. Seeking challenge, showing a 'can do' attitude. Taking a risk, engaging in new experiences, and learning by trial and error.	The characteristics are used by the practitioner to guide the analysis of the observations of Adam. See pages 27–29 and 31–32.
Active Learning *motivation*	**Being involved and concentrating** Maintaining focus on their activity for a period of time. Showing high levels of energy, fascination, not easily distracted and paying attention to details. **Keeping on trying** Persisting with activity when challenges occur. Showing a belief that more effort or a different approach will pay off. Bouncing back after difficulties. **Enjoying achieving what they set out to do** Showing satisfaction in meeting their own goals, being proud of how they accomplished something (not just the end result). Enjoying meeting challenges for their own sake rather than external rewards or praise.	
Creating and Thinking *critically thinking*	**Having their own ideas** Thinking of ideas, finding ways to solve problems, finding new ways to do things. **Making links** Making links and noticing patterns in their experience, making predictions and testing their ideas. Developing ideas of grouping, sequences, cause-and-effect. **Choosing ways to do things** Planning, making decisions about how to approach a task, solve a problem and reach a goal, checking how well their activities are progressing. Changing strategies as needed and reviewing how well the approach worked.	

Source: Stewart, 2011

Child's Name: Adam

Start Date: January 2013

PSED

DOB: 16.09.09

First Language: English/Somali

Keyperson: Rosalyn

Stages of develop.	Making relationships	Self confidence and self awareness	Managing feelings and behaviour
8–20 mts	Children seek to gain attention in a variety of ways. They build relationships with special people and are wary of those they do not know. They interact with others and explore new situations when supported by a familiar person. They show interest in the activities of others. Developing – 12.02.13/ Secure – 27.03.13	Children enjoy finding their own nose, eyes or tummy in naming games. They learn that their own voice and actions have an effect on others. They use pointing with eye gaze to make requests and to share an interest. They engage another person to help them achieve a goal e.g. to get an object which is out of reach.	Children use a familiar adult to share feelings like excitement or pleasure, and for comfort when tired or distressed. They have a growing ability to soothe themselves, and may use a comfort object. They cooperate with care routines like getting dressed. They are beginning to understand 'yes', 'no' and some boundaries.
16–24 mts	Children play alongside others and use familiar adults as a 'secure base'. They play cooperatively with a familiar adult.	Children explore new toys and environments, 'checking in' with a familiar adult when they need to. They are beginning to be able to take part in pretend play. They demonstrate a sense of self as an individual, e.g. wanting to do things independently, saying 'no'.	Children are aware of the feelings of other people. They have a growing sense of will and determination which may result in feelings of anger and frustration at times. They respond to a few appropriate boundaries with encouragement and support. They are beginning to learn that some things are theirs, some are shared, and some belong to others.
22–36 mts	Children are interested in others' play and starting to join in; they seek out others to share experiences with. Children show affection and concern for people who are special to them and may form a special friendship with another child. Developing – 12.02.13/ Secure – 27.03.13	Children separate from main carer with support and encouragement from a familiar adult; they are able to expresses own preferences and interests. Developing – 12.02.13 / Secure – 27.02.13	Children seek comfort from familiar adults when needed and can express their own feelings such as sad, happy, cross, scared, worried. They respond to the feelings and wishes of others. Children are aware that some actions can hurt or harm others; they try to help or give comfort when others are distressed. They show understanding and cooperate with some boundaries and routines. Children can manage their own actions/behaviours, e.g. stopping themselves from doing something they shouldn't do. They have a growing ability to distract themselves when upset, e.g. by engaging in a new play activity. Emerging – 12.02.13/ Developing – 27.03.13/ Secure – 27.06.13

Stages of develop.	Making relationships	Self confidence and self awareness	Managing feelings and behaviour
30–50 mts	Children play as part of a group and know how to make friends with others. They can initiate play with other children and keep it going. They show some awareness of other children's needs. Emerging – 27.06.13 Secure – 06.12.13	Children select and use resources with support and value praise for what they have done. They enjoy responsibility for carrying out small tasks. They are more confident with new people and in new situations. They talk confidently to other children in play, and talk freely about home and community. Emerging – 27.06.13/ Secure – 06.12.13	Children are aware of their own feelings and know that some actions and words can hurt others' feelings. They can take turns and share, sometimes with support from others. They can usually manage to wait when their needs are not immediately met, and can usually adapt their behaviour to different events, social situations and changes in routine.
40–60 mts	Children initiate conversation, are able to attend to others and take into account what others are saying. Children are able to explain their reasoning, own knowledge and understanding and ask appropriate questions of others. They will make attempts to resolve conflicts with other children and are able to compromise.	Children are confident to speak to others about their own needs, wants interests and opinions, they can describe themselves in positive terms and talk about their own abilities.	Children understand that their own actions affect other people, they are aware of boundaries set and of behavioural expectations in the setting. Children are beginning to be able to negotiate and solve problems appropriately between themselves.
Early Learning Goal	**Children play cooperatively, taking turns with others. They take account of one another's ideas about how to organise their activity. They show sensitivity to others' needs and feelings, and form positive relationships with adults and other children.**	**Children are confident to try new activities and say why they like some activities more than others. They are confident to speak in a familiar group, will talk about their ideas and will choose the resources they need for their chosen activities. They say when they do or do not need help.**	**Children talk about how they and others show feelings, talk about their own and others' behaviour and its consequences, and know that some behaviour is unacceptable. They work as part of a group or class and understand and follow the rules. They adjust their behaviour to different situations, and take changes of routine in their stride.**

Communication and Language

Stages of develop.	Listening and attention	Understanding	Speaking
8–20 mts	Children move their body to sounds they enjoy, such as music or a regular beat. They have a strong exploratory impulse and can concentrate intently on an object or activity of their own choosing for short periods. They pay attention to a dominant stimulus.	Children select familiar objects by name and will go and find objects when asked, or identify objects from a group. They understand simple sentences like 'throw the ball.'	Children use sounds in play e.g. 'brmm' for a toy car. They use single words and frequently imitate words and sounds. They enjoy babbling and increasingly experiment with using sound and words to communicate for a range of purposes. They use pointing with eye gaze to make requests and to share an interest. They create their own 'personal words' as they begin to develop language.
16–24 mts	Children listen to and enjoy rhythmic patterns in rhymes and stories. They enjoy rhymes and demonstrate listening by trying to join in with actions or vocalisations. They have 'rigid attention' and may seem not to hear when they are engaged in something.	Children can select familiar objects by name and will go and find objects when asked, or identify objects from a group. Children understand simple sentences (e.g. 'throw the ball').	Children use language to widen contacts and share experiences, feelings and thoughts. They can hold a conversation but may jump from topic to topic. They learn new words very rapidly and are able to use them in communicating. They use gestures, sometimes with talk. They ask a variety of questions (*what, where, who?*) and have limited use of simple sentences (e.g. 'mummy gonna work'). They are beginning to use word endings (e.g. *going, cats*).
22–36 mts	Children listen with interest to the noises adults make when they read stories; they recognise and respond to many familiar sounds, e.g. turning to a knock on the door, looking at or going to the door. Children show an interest in play with sounds, songs and rhymes. Children's attention is mainly single channelled; they can shift to a different task if their attention is fully obtained – using the child's name helps focus.	Children can identify action words by pointing to the right picture, e.g. '*Who's jumping?*' and they understand more complex sentences, e.g. '*Put your toys away and then we'll read a book.*' Children understand 'who', 'what', 'where' in simple questions (e.g. *Who's that? What's that? Where is?*) and are developing an understanding of simple concepts (e.g. *big/ little*).	Children use language as a powerful means of widening contacts, sharing feelings, experiences and thoughts. They can hold a conversation, jumping from topic to topic, and learn new words very rapidly, gradually becoming able to use them in communicating. Children use gestures, sometimes with limited talk, e.g. reaches toward toy, saying '*I have it*' as well as a variety of questions (e.g. *what, where, who*). Children use simple sentences (e.g. '*Mummy gonna work.*') and are beginning to use work endings (e.g. *going, cats*).

Secure – 12.2.13 |

Stages of develop.	Listening and attention	Understanding	Speaking
30–50 mts	Children listen to others one-to-one or in small groups when the conversation interests them. They listen to stories with increasing attention and recall, and join in with repeated refrains and phrases in rhymes and stories. They can focus their attention – still listening or doing, but they can shift their own attention. They can follow directions if not intently focused on what they are doing. Emerging – 12.2.13/Developing – 27.6.13	Children understand the use of objects. They show practical understanding of prepositions like under, on top or behind. They can respond to simple instructions and are beginning to understand 'how' and 'why' questions. Emerging – 12.2.13/ Developing – 22.3.13 Secure – 27.6.13	Children are beginning to use more complex sentences with words like 'and' or 'because'. They can retell a simple event in order. They use talk to connect ideas, explain what is happening and what might happen next, and recall past experiences. They can ask questions using words like 'who', 'what', 'when', 'how' and can give explanations. They use tenses to talk about the past, present and future. They can use intonation, rhythm and phrasing to make their meaning clear and can use vocabulary focused on objects and people that are of special importance. Their vocabulary is growing to reflect the breadth of their experiences. They use talk to pretend that one thing stands for another. Emerging – 22.3.13/ Developing – 22.06.13
40–60 mts	Children maintain attention, concentrate and sit quietly when appropriate to the situation. Children can attend to two things at one time, for example they can listen to others while continuing to build with blocks or paint a picture. Developing – 06.12.13	Children respond to instructions involving a two-part sequence; they understand humour, for example nonsense rhymes and jokes. They are able to follow a story without visual aids and props and are able to listen and respond to ideas expressed by others in conversation. Developing – 06.12.13	Children extend their vocabulary, especially by grouping and naming, exploring the meaning and sounds of new words. They use language to imagine and recreate roles and experiences in play situations. Children link statements and stick to a main theme or intention in conversation. They use talk to organise, sequence and clarify thinking, ideas feelings and events. Developing – 06.06.13
Early Learning Goal	**Children listen attentively in a range of situations. They listen to stories, accurately anticipating key events and responding to what they hear with relevant comments, questions or actions. They give their attention to what others say and respond appropriately, while engaged in another activity.**	**Children follow instructions involving several ideas or actions. They answer 'how' or 'why' questions about their experiences in response to stories or events.**	**Children express themselves effectively, showing awareness of listeners needs. They use past, present and future forms accurately when talking about events that have happened or are to happen in the future. They develop their own narrative and explanations by connecting ideas or events.**

Figure 3.9 Adam's assessment for learning record

> ## What we have learned
>
> - Developing the skill of observing is important.
> - Where possible, non-contact time can enable practitioners to have sufficient time to reflect and discuss observations and their interpretations.
> - How structuring the learning environment is important.
> - How at Vanessa Nursery School the staff make regular systematic observations of each child.
> - The importance of on-going, purposeful, planned and spontaneous observations.

Alexander, his parents, and his keyperson Jemma

We have seen how Adam's mother, Nima, has a good relationship with his keyperson, Rosalyn, who is a teacher at the school.

Alexander's keyperson is called Jemma, who has been trained as an Early Years Educator. His parents are architects, so they both work, and Alexander has a nanny as part of the team. This means that Jemma needs to work closely with both the nanny and Alexander's parents. Alexander has special educational needs. He is beginning to learn to use a walker, which is increasing his mobility and giving him the possibility of making more choices. He is also beginning to be able to point to pictures in his communication book to show what he wants. The learning support assistant who supports him follows the recommendations of the occupational therapist, the physiotherapist and the speech and language therapist. The keyperson is important here in ensuring that this group of adults, all with differing training backgrounds, work together positively and in ways which do not contradict each other's recommendations. Jemma is the very experienced practitioner who fulfils this role.

During the weekly planning sessions, Jemma makes sure that Alexander's Individual Education Plan (IEP) is referred to and acted on, as well as looking at the general provision that Alexander needs. The whole nursery team are aware of the targets (which the nursery staff prefer to call learning intentions) that Alexander is working towards.

Because of the careful and sensitive work of his keyperson, Jemma, Alexander has begun (his Statutory Annual Review Record shows) to 'settle into his key group in the nursery. He is beginning to enjoy accessing different learning experiences during his time at nursery.'

There is a summary of the views of the parents following regular meetings of the team who support Alexander on the form below. Parents need to feel that they are part of the team.

Summary of parent(s)'/carer(s)' views presented verbally at meetings

Alexander's mother, Joanna, was happy that Alexander has settled at nursery. She was keen that he continues to access the various therapies that he has been attending. She does not want to lose the therapeutic input that Alexander has benefitted from.

We discussed how some of Alexander's non-educational targets could be included in his IEP and some of them would be provided for Alexander beyond the nursery. We have also discussed the importance of Alexander accessing the English EYFS curriculum while he attends a mainstream nursery school.

We also noticed that there is not any specific mention of Alexander's physiotherapy needs on his Statement. Joanna feels that this needs to be addressed immediately as Alexander needs a good deal of input from the physiotherapist.

The variety of terminology that arises between differently trained professionals is a challenge. Early childhood practitioners, such as teachers and Early Years Educators, need to be bilingual as a minimum, as we shall see in the chapter on children with ASD (see Chapter 6). Therapists tend to use terms such as 'targets', whereas early childhood practitioners prefer to talk about 'learning intentions'. The medical profession are not usually prepared to change their terminology because they need to fill in forms with required terms, but there does not need to be a problem providing early childhood practitioners are able to switch from one to the other. This will give rise to fascinating discussions in all probability.

An example of this need for discussion about the terminology preferred by different professionals is Alexander's Individual Education Plan: Early Years Action Plus. The agreed learning intention, that he should 'interact with the children', is called a SMART target on his IEP.

What we have learned

A summary of the session:

- Home visits are an important way of establishing a relaxed, positive relationship between parents and practitioners.
- Books around the nursery which help parents to understand the key messages about the education of their child are helpful because they make tangible aspects of learning mathematics, for example through blockplay.

(Continued)

(Continued)

- Observations of children engaged in various situations at different times of day help to create a picture of their learning.
- Parents need to be involved and to feel they are part of the team working with their child.
- Parents need to understand that various professionals have different terminology, but the keyperson and SENCO need to be professionally bilingual so that there is no conflict of approach and discussions can genuinely tease out issues about the best ways of supporting a child's learning and working well together.
- Not everything needs to be written down. It is the significant markers that need to be documented.

Reflections on this chapter

- Parents need to feel that they can trust the staff they work with. At Vanessa Nursery School the Headteacher, Deputy Headteacher (who is the SENCO), and the two keypersons (who are a teacher and an early years professional) are all trusted. This has resulted in the facilitation of and great quality in the education of the children.
- Review your partnerships and ways of working with parents/carers. What works well, and what is less successful? What could you do differently to improve your relationships?

Further reading

Bruce, T. (2011) *Learning Through Play: Babies, Toddlers and Young Children* (2nd edn). London: Hodder.

Isaacs, S. (1930) *Intellectual Growth in Young Children*. London: Routledge and Kegan Paul.

CHAPTER 4

FROM BABY TO TODDLER

> **In this chapter you will learn about:**
>
> - The importance of the partnership with parents in observing and acting on observation to support a baby's journey into being a toddler.
> - The value of observation that illuminates practice when various experts pool their knowledge and work together.

Setting the context

The building and the community who use the building

The Ann Bernadt Nursery School and Children's Centre (previously called Sumner Nursery School) is set in the heart of Peckham in London. There is a close community, and many of the parents at the school attended it when they were children. It is a very diverse population, and the nursery school is an important part of the community, with an excellent reputation. The garden is large, and each class has an allotment at the edge of the garden.

The nursery school is built in the traditional design pioneered by Margaret MacMillan, who invented 'nursery schools' at the turn of the nineteenth century. The school was one of the first nursery schools in London in the early 1900s. The classrooms are, as is typical of the design, in a row, with a door opening onto a shelter which is exposed to the elements. This allows children to be out of doors in inclement weather, and they are able to be involved in woodwork, wooden blockplay, sand play, and many more educationally worthwhile experiences in any weather, be it snow or hail, sleet or a heat wave. Children who wish to may also go beyond the shelter into an area that is completely out in the open air.

The doors for each classroom inside the building open onto the hall. Children eat in this hall, but the space is used for a variety of activities during the day. On the opposite side of the hall there are the offices, a kitchen and a room for children under three years of age, with a garden accessed through doors from other rooms. The classic design of this building has stood the test of time. It works.

The Triangle of Trust: child, parent and practitioner

It is important to introduce the Triangle of Trust developed by Peter Elfer, Elinor Goldschmied and Dorothy Selleck (2012), which is discussed with great clarity by Peter Elfer in the Siren film *The Two Year Old*. If parents do not have a sense of trust in their child's keyperson then any records kept of that child's progress will not hold any meaning that is useful for them to have. There may even be some doubt on the part of the parent about the accuracy of such records.

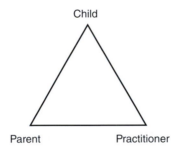

Figure 4.1   The Triangle of Trust (source: Goldschmied and Selleck, 1996: 12)

Parents need to feel able to trust the people with whom they leave their child. They also need to know that this person will not attempt to take their place as parents from them and to feel reassured that the keyperson will not do this unwittingly. They need to be confident that the ways in which they develop together in 'handing over' the child are right for them as a family, for the parents and for the child.

In this chapter, we shall see how the Triangle of Trust is a crucial part of the way that records for the progress of one child, Kaya, are kept.

How the staff work

Keyperson

It is vital not to see the keyperson (a legally enshrined requirement in the English context in the Early Years Foundation Stage) as the only person who works with a child as that is not the idea at all:

A keyperson has special responsibilities for working with a number of children, giving them reassurance to feel safe and cared for and building relationships with their parent carers. (EYFS Practice Card 2.4: 'Positive Relationships – Keyperson')

The keyperson helps a baby or child to settle, and to feel safe and confident, talks with the parent/carers so as to make sure that the needs of their child are being met appropriately, and makes sure that the records of development and progress are shared regularly with the parents (and other professionals when necessary). The keyperson makes a vital contribution to the creation of an atmosphere in which each child can thrive, and in which there is a Triangle of Trust between the child, parents and practitioner. Good team work with colleagues is a key part of bringing this about.

At Ann Bernadt, Yerebri is the keyperson for Kaya. She stresses the importance of the team when working with children and making a good partnership with parents. She has been based in under-threes work, and this is how she came to work with Kaya.

Kaya began to attend the Ann Bernadt Centre when she was nine months old. Her mother, Marcia, is an experienced parent, with three older children, two of whom had attended Ann Bernadt in the nursery school some years previously. There is a wide gap in age between the older children and Kaya.

When she began to attend Ann Bernadt, Kaya could only sit with support and she did not crawl or walk. She had skin problems which presented in a similar way to having burns. She found it unbearable to be touched, and was nervous in the company of other children. She was, as Yerebri describes her, fragile. Kaya's mother was understandably very concerned about her daughter. She came to Ann Bernadt hoping to find help. She needed to work full-time, and so required a daycare place for her small daughter. She was anxious about leaving her, and also anxious about finding ways to help her. She had had good experiences with her older children attending the nursery school, but this was a different situation. Kaya was not quite one year old, and she was in difficulty because of her painful skin and lack of mobility.

Involving health experts

At Ann Bernadt, it was suggested to Kaya's mother that she should seek help from her GP. She did this, grateful for the suggestion. When parents are dealing with challenging situations, they are usually appreciative of this kind of help. It is difficult to think straight when living day on day with a child in pain and the necessity of going to work. The GP set up allergy tests and the result was that Kaya was found to have a variety of allergies: these included household dust, dairy products, gluten, and bread fibre.

Involving the cook at Ann Bernadt: a revolution in diet to tackle the allergies

Once the food allergies had been identified, the cook worked with the key-person and the under-threes team to ensure that Kaya's diet was revolution-ised such that the foods to which she was allergic were excluded. Her diet was altered to fruit, vegetables, pulses (such as soya beans), rice, gluten-free bread and gluten-free pasta. At first there did not appear to be any improve-ment, but a slow and gradual change then began to take place.

Teamwork in adapting the physical environment

Because Kaya was also allergic to dust, staff wore protective covers over their shoes to keep the floors as clean as possible and minimise dust. It was also important to make sure that the sleeping arrangements were carefully consid-ered. A special cover and bedding were introduced for Kaya to sleep on. However, if the environment had become too clinically clean Kaya may not have built up some of the antibodies that were vital to living in a normal world. She would not then have been able to experience everyday life. There was therefore a balancing act required in providing the optimum physical environment for her.

Over a period of about six months, Kaya began to sleep better. Staff were anxious at first, and so kept checking her breathing when she fell asleep.

She began to enjoy using her hands and holding her spoon as she ate. She wanted to hold toys. She joined in the messy paint play, and chose to play with the sand.

At the end of the six month period Kaya was able to sit unaided. Perhaps this was because the pressure on different parts of her body, which are a natural part of sitting, did not cause her such pain. Once she could sit, her physical strength began to build. She did not crawl easily, and when she did she dragged her leg and scooted on one knee to avoid contact on the ground as much as possible. She preferred to 'cruise' from one bit of furniture to the next, and gradually man-aged to make a few tottering steps without holding on to any furniture.

Keeping the Triangle of Trust

There were daily contact and discussions between Kaya's mother and her keyperson Yerebri. This however did not mean that other staff would not also talk about Kaya's progress and learning as it was a team effort. Yerebri was constantly concerned that although she was Kaya's keyperson she did not feel that the progress made by Kaya during the six months was something she should take all the credit for. Her professional attitude shows the maturity that comes when a practitioner is as pleased with the contribution of colleagues as with the part they have played in helping a child to develop and learn.

Another indication of Yerebri's professionalism was her insight into her practice. She recognised when she needed support from her colleagues. She found it difficult to help Kaya to feed in the early stages. She preferred to talk about her desire for a connection with children rather than attachment. Time and again she stressed the importance of staff recognising each others' strengths, and helping them where they did not feel so strong. An atmosphere of working with children which encourages practitioners to acknowledge their weaker areas benefits children and familiies. Otherwise the practice can easily become defensive, or complacent and arrogant. There is a difference between over-claiming the quality of the practice, and the quiet taking of pleasure, satisfaction and pride in the progress of a child. The stronger the practice, the more practitioners are aware of what is going well and what needs to be addressed. Professional insight is of central importance.

Marcia, Kaya's mother, described how the staff at Ann Bernadt were emotionally available to her and Kaya. She recalls them as being patient, observant and flexible in their approach to understanding which dairy product was triggering Kaya's eczema: 'They worked tirelessly as we tried together to figure out what was causing Kaya's eczema and how to prevent it from coming back'.

The staff had a range of strategies to observe and support Kaya when she was uncomfortable in her own skin. Marcia explains how they worked in partnership with her to ensure that Kaya was kept as comfortable as possible. They would apply cream and administer medication prescribed by her GP. Marcia was asked by the staff to bring in spare cotton clothing for Kaya to change into. The staff observed her breathing and reactions, and the room temperature was monitored to ensure that she was kept cool. Marcia also explained how their valuable insights about Kaya's development and the development of her immune system helped her to support her daughter to be more independent at home, where she could see that she was developing rapidly.

Marcia describes how she had regular access to Kaya's records, which were located by the door as she entered the room. These enabled her to see fascinating observations about Kaya's life at nursery: for example, her love of books, particularly *Brown Bear*, which Marcia purchased a copy of from a local bookshop. In this way she was able to complement what was already happening at the nursery. Marcia explained how she felt involved and valued by the team, resulting in her feeling confident enough to leave Kaya. She knew that the staff would attend to her daughter's needs and that she was secure with Yerebri. What was important here was that Marcia felt she could go to work in the knowledge that if Kaya's skin flared up the staff would contact her.

Relationships with other children

As Kaya made progress in her walking, she wanted to do as the other children did. Children at around 18 months are very aware of what other children are doing. She wanted to go outside into the garden if they did. It took her longer to walk out there, but she was determined, and managed it. There were about seven children in the group, ranging from one to two years of age. She was, although not the youngest, the smallest. The other children seemed to recognise that she needed more time to reach places, and they were very sensitive to her, sensing that she needed care. They nurtured her. This resonates with the observations that Vivian Gussin Paley made in her book about two year olds, *The Kindness of Children*, but children are only kind and nurturing towards each other when they are treated with respect and feel cared for.

There are several significant aspects that emerged here:

- The new diet led to the lessening and near disappearance of the skin problem. This came as a result of the interventions from health experts.
- The release from pain that this brought allowed Kaya to move more freely, so that she began to gain in strength. Her physical development was no longer constrained, and she began to follow the biologically normal route of sitting, crawling and walking, as well as developing the use of her hands.
- Adaptations in the physical environment kept dust to a level where Kaya was able to join in with play with toys and other materials (e.g. paint) and, crucially, to sleep better. She could hold books with her hands, and the records of her progress frequently showed her looking, with great engagement, at a book.
- Kaya's social interactions and relationships with staff and other children made great progress. Once she could be held and cuddled without pain, it was easier for her to relate to Yerebri and the team of practitioners. She could also join other children in their play, in their experiences with toys, paint and sand, and enjoy their company without the fear of painful physical contact.

Because Kaya was being educated in England, her development and learning at Ann Bernadt were approached through the Early Years Foundation Stage which was legally enshrined in 2012. The Local Authority developed the STAR Record of Achievement (Southwark Transition and Assessment Record) to address the earlier form of the EYFS. This has a section for the settling-in of each child, and other sections for each area of development and learning.

New ways of recording observations

There has been a period of transition in the Local Authority into a new way of recording observations. The aim is to reduce paperwork, but to keep quality in the observations and the way they inform assessment and planning.

Oliver's record, shown on the next few pages, is in the new format. Here we can see that one observation can be used to note what he is engaged in, and to assess his progress in the different areas of development and learning across time. The characteristics of learning are also noted.

Oliver's Record of Achievement

Observation Sheet 1

Figure 4.2   Oliver 1 – home corner

Oliver was exploring the home corner. He was trying to draw the attention of an adult to see what he was doing.

Figure 4.3   Oliver 2 – comfortable area

Oliver was sitting in the comfortable area exploring a book.

Figure 4.4   Oliver 3 – sand area

Oliver was playing with sand in the sand area. He was using the spade to put some sand in the bucket and putting it back.

Figure 4.5   Oliver 4 – engaged paint

Oliver was engaged in his activity. He was enjoying the sensory experience. He dumps paint on his paper.

(Continued)

(Continued)

Figure 4.6   Oliver 5 – wooden spoon

Oliver is role playing in the kitchen; he has just finished cooking. He is opening the pot and stirring with a wooden spoon.

Planned observation

Oliver is sitting on the mat in the quite area looking at a book and pointing to a duck. He looks up to an adult and says 'quack, quack.' He continues to open other pages babbling some words. Oliver closes the book and opens it again, and points at the duck saying 'quack, quack.' He gets up and picks up a duck toy which he gives to an adult and he says 'quack quack'. The adult presses the duck toy which produces the 'quack, quack' sound. Oliver listens to the sound that the duck toy makes and begins to smile.

Observation Sheet 2

Figure 4.7   Oliver 6 – doll

Oliver is playing pretend with the doll. He is babbling and smiling with the doll.

Figure 4.8   Oliver 7 – musical instrument

Oliver is playing with his friend during Circle Time. He is banging the drum with another musical instrument.

Planned observation

Oliver was playing in the home corner with the musical toy. He was exploring the toy by trying to produce a sound from it. He took the CD by the computer and put it in the appropriate place. He then closed the compartment and started to press the buttons on the player but no sound was produced. He got up and went to the construction area to do some construction work for a while and went back to continue with the musical toy. He continued pressing all of the buttons on the toy until he got the right button. When the toy started singing, Oliver was shaking his head to the music. He continued to press for different music.

Figure 4.9   Oliver 8 – musical instrument

Oliver is exploring a musical toy in the home corner by pressing the buttons to produce sounds.

In Figure 4.9, Oliver is enjoying exploring a musical instrument. The observation focuses on this. The practitioner has written down the detail of what happened. This example can then be used to identify both the areas of development and learning and the Characteristics of Learning.

The prime areas are:

- Personal, social and emotional development (PSED).
- Physical development (PD).
- Communication and language (CL).

The specific areas are:

- Literacy.
- Mathematics.
- Understanding the world.
- Expressive art and design.

The characteristics of learning are:

- Playing and exploring.
- Finding out and exploring.
- Children playing with what they know.
- Being willing to have a go.

Active learning encompasses:

- Being involved and concentrating.
- Keeping trying.
- Children enjoying and achieving what they set out to do.

Creating and thinking critically encompasses:

- Children having their own ideas.
- Making links.
- Choosing ways to do things.

Kaya enjoys books

The following examples from Kaya's Record of Achievement show her enjoyment of books. There are photographs of her deeply involved in looking at books, and the record notes:

> [Kaya] concentrates intently on a book of her own choosing for a short period.

This develops, so that she sometimes feels comfortable having another child next to her while she looks at a book. They share the book:

Figure 4.10   Kaya with another child

Kaya has now moved on from *Brown Bear* to a new book, *Dear Zoo*, which she fetched from the book box each time she came into the book area. Happy to look through it alone or with another child by her side.

Another observation, three months later, states:

Kaya enjoys short repetitive story books. She can sit

quietly with an adult or alone to look through a known book or listen to the adult. She can also recreate a scenario and use props to match the story. She fetched the toy near and put him beside *Brown Bear*.

The following month Kaya showed that her language was developing rapidly:

Kaya fetches a book with various pictures of vehicles. She moves from the book area and chooses to sit in the middle of the room. She opens the book and different transport images appear. She looks closely (studying the page) and points to a picture and says with an excited voice, 'car, wroom, wroom'.

Two months later:

Kaya led a pretend play in the home corner. She filled a bowl with some dry pasta, gave it to a child nearby and said, 'eat, yours, pasta'.

Four months further on the records describe how:

Kaya plays in a home corner. She puts on the kettle and says, 'Who want a tea?' When nobody responds 'Ho, so, they don't want drink tea'.

Each of these observations has been colour-coded and matched to an age from 'Development Matters'. The age links to the child's progress and can be gathered into a chart showing which aspects of achievement are at the level of 'emerging', 'developing' or 'secure' in the prime areas and the specific areas of development and learning. Each age group is colour-coded. This means that it is easy to spot where the child is operating: below their chronological age, at that age, or beyond it.

Kaya's colour-coded chart shows how in some respects she is functioning at the earlier levels. But in other respects her development and learning are at a later level. This shows clearly the way that development and learning are uneven, with plateaux and times of rapid progression.

By the time she is two years old, her development and learning is mainly in the 22–36 months period. Her love of patterns and delight in comparing quantities, and her grasp of the language of time, linked to the here and now, suggest that in these areas she is functioning at the 30–50 months level by the time she is moving to the nursery school from the under-threes section of Ann Bernadt.

This is a very encouraging situation. The records show that Kaya, despite her difficult start caused by her allergies, has made rapid and impressive progress during her time at Ann Bernadt. She has, quite literally, caught up. The early intervention worked. The records demonstrate this. It is very important that records show observations which can inform assessment and planning. They must also show the child's journey of development and learning. This means they should plot progress and give evidence of it.

Figure 4.11   Blockplay sequence

What we have learned

In this chapter, it is clear that Kaya has made excellent progress. How do we know?

- The Record of Achievement has observations with photographs and notes. These are used to inform the assessment and the planning of Kaya's development and learning. They are linked to the document 'Development

Matters' so that her learning is related to her age group. They inform whether her learning is emerging, developing or secure. They help staff to think about what is next.

- The records are shared with her mother regularly, but they make more sense to her when she sees them because of the daily chats she has with Kaya's Keyperson in particular, but also with other staff, when she brings and fetches Kaya.
- We see Kaya as a whole child. Her health has a huge impact on her ability to learn. With the right specialist help from a range of professionals, and a triangle of trust with the keyperson, Kaya has been able to flourish, and to make the transition to the nursery school with good heath and well being.

Reflections on this chapter

- Have a think about the Triangle of Trust. Is it embedded in your setting? Would Kaya have been able to make the progress she did without it? What will you do about the Triangle of Trust in your setting as a result of reading this chapter?

Further reading

Elfer, P., Goldschmied, E. and Selleck, D. (2012) *Keypersons in the Early Years: Building Relationships for Quality Provision in Early Years Settings and Primary Schools* (2nd edn). London: David Fulton.

Forbes, R. (2004) *Beginning to Play.* Maidenhead: Open University Press.

Hughes, A. (2012) *Building Relationships with Parents of Young Children: A Guide to Effective Communication.* London: Routledge.

DVDs

Siren Films, *The Two Year Old,* www.sirenfilms.co.uk

Siren Films *Physical development,* www.sirenfilms.co.uk

Discovered Treasure: The Life and Work of Elinor Goldschmied 1910–2009, The Froebel Trust, www.froebeltrust.og.uk

Froebel Early Childhood Archive Collection, Roehampton Digital Collection, University of Roehampton.

CHAPTER 5

USING SCHEMAS AS A LENS

In this chapter you will learn about:

- Schemas and their practical use as an observational technique.
- The importance of sharing and acting on observations with the family both when children are settling-in and as they continue the learning journey.

The setting

Barbados Playgroup, Hampshire, is an exemplary case of a playgroup that has not lost the spirit of the founder of the Playgroup Movement in the 1960s, Belle Tutaev, OBE. It is at the heart of its community, and some of the children attending are nieces, nephews and grandchildren of the playgroup staff who lead it. Its spirit is apparent in the two words 'play' and 'group'.

There is pressure, through government and local authority policy, for the day to be extended from mornings-only to full daycare. The reason put forward for this is often that it would allow parents, especially mothers, to work. Playgroups were founded so that children could play together, which is still very important in rural areas, and where, in urban situations, it is hard for parents to meet.

The staff at Barbados wisely recognise that the quality is there because what they offer to the children and families works best as a half day and not a full day. It is rare to see such quality nowadays, especially when children so often spend long hours in daycare. At Barbados, the children are tired at the end of the morning, and they know they can come to the mat at the end of the session and go home happy, tired and fulfilled. Their well-being is high as they walk down the street afterwards with their families/carers. It is heartening to see children having the sort of educational experiences which will stay with them throughout their lives. Because these are half-day sessions, the staff are able to give thought to the planning and preparation, and they have the time at the end of the morning to discuss and reflect together so as to get the most out of the time they spend with the children each day.

The Playgroup Movement, founded in the 1960s, originally had two aspects – the child and the parents. The parents and families were involved in being trained to offer the provision, usually mornings only, and not necessarily every day. A parent committee led and reviewed the provision. Molly Brearley was the Principal of the Froebel Educational Institute, and in the late 1960s, the Institute offered training for the tutors training playgroup leaders. Traditionally, playgroups have taken a Froebelian approach. This means that they emphasise the importance of play in the development of young children's learning. They also place great emphasis on the social and emotional development of young children and their families. They value the whole child – 'making the inner outer and the outer inner', as the pioneer educator Friedrich Froebel described this. This means they provide a physical environment which offers rich sensory experiences to children both indoors and out of doors. The words 'play' and 'group' are significant and important in the original title of the organisation.

Some thirty years on from its founding, there was a split in the Playgroup Movement. A central organisation was formed, although some groups remained as independent playgroups. In 1995 the organisation became the Pre-School Learning Alliance. This title evokes a different meaning.

Barbados is located in a large hall. The furniture and storage are designed to be multi-purpose so that the hall can be used for other purposes. The outdoor space is large and on a very exciting slope, quite steep in places, which is greatly appealing to children. There is also a flat section at the bottom for flatter activities. The area is easy for adults to oversee, and yet children have nooks and corners to explore.

The Early Years Foundation Stage – Barbados Playgroup

Every setting in England follows the legally enshrined Early Years Foundation Stage Framework, known as the EYFS. However, since 2000 there have been three frameworks in England, with the first two – *Curriculum Guidance for the Foundation Stage* (DfEE/QCA, 2000) and *Birth to Three Matters* (DfES, 2002) – being the best. The key to getting the most out of official frameworks is to begin with the child, so that the document is not used prescriptively and it doesn't over-dominate. Observation that is informed by knowledge and understanding of child development is the key. Once adults have tuned into the child, they can select what is appropriate from official documents and get the most out of them.

At Barbados, as one of their observation strategies, the staff use schemas to guide them into their work with the children, and to help them conform to the legal requirements of the EYFS.

Schemas

> A schema is a pattern of repeatable behaviour into which experiences are assimilated and that are gradually coordinated. Coordinations lead to higher-level and more powerful schemas. (Athey, 1990: 37)

At first, schemas are part of the brain's development through the senses and movements of the baby and toddler. Gradually, as symbolic behaviour emerges, the toddler begins to walk, talk and pretend. During this phase, we also begin to see early cause-and-effect relationships developing. One of the reasons why it is so exciting to work with two year olds is that there is an explosion of language, pretend play and efforts to work out what causes what to happen. So many things are emerging at the same time. The excellent 'Birth to Three Matters' document (DfES, 2002) which is still, very sensibly and understandably, used by practitioners, describes the fact that walking, talking and pretending often come together. The transition from babyhood demands huge energy on the part of the child. Two year olds quickly become over excited and easily frustrated as they are on the edge of so much learning, and wanting to do everything 'now'. They need to spend time with adults who understand their needs, and who can help them get stuck into their learning and flourish.

Many of the children at Barbados are two years old. This means that they are not yet at the stage where adults can easily tune into their development and learning through listening to what they say. The emphasis needs to be on observing what they do, and then helping children to expand their vocabulary and possibly articulate and expand their thinking through language. Schemas are invaluable in working with two year olds for this reason:

> Babies and young children learn from their first hand experiences, and they will use their repeated experiences to help them to practise, remember and organise their ideas, as they link them with their previous experiences. (Louis et al. 2013: 19)

Knowing about schemas helps adults working with very young children to tune into each child but this also informs the planning. It helps the adult to work out whether a child needs more of the same (often the case) or to extend the learning by expanding it.

> The key to good learning is for the adult to:
>
> 'OBSERVE, SUPPORT AND EXPAND THE LEARNING'. (Bruce, 2011: 216)

In this chapter, we will explore this process through getting to know two children, Billy and Katie-anne. We will see their schemas, and how the staff use their observations to inform their planning.

How the team works

Before starting at Barbados Playgroup, every child receives a **home visit.** The keyperson fills in a 'home profile' with the family (Figure 5.1).

BARBADOS PLAYGROUP LTD

HOME VISIT PROFILE

CHILD'S NAME:

....

Date of birth   _____

Home address   _____

            _____

            _____

            _____

Telephone no.   _____

Date of home visit   _____

Parents' names   _____

Age of child on entry   _____

Who has parental responsibility?   _____

Data Protection Act: The personal data you supply will be used for the purpose for which you have provided it and any relevant procedures following from this. This data will be maintained in accordance with the Act and will not be shared with other organisations or disclosed to anyone else without your prior consent unless we are required by law to do so.

(Continued)

(Continued)

Child's position in family _____

Language spoken at home / culture / customs / religion

Who will bring your child to school and collect them at the end of the day?

How close is family to you? How often do you see them?

What sort of activities (as a family) happens? How often?

HEALTH

Birth weight _____

Any birth problems? (please list)

Name of family doctor/health visitor

Have you any concerns about your child's:
(If yes please give more details)

Hearing?

Eyesight?

Mobility?

Speech?

Behaviour?

Does your child sleep through the night, in their own bed?

What kinds of food do they like to eat?

Can they use cutlery to eat with? Can they chew their food?

Are the family mealtimes together at a table?

Does he/she attend a hospital or clinic for regular treatment?

(Continued)

(Continued)

LIKES AND DISLIKES

Has your child attended any other kind of setting?   Y   N

What kind of setting is/was it?

Did he/she enjoy it?   Y   N

What did he/she like best?

How does he/she react to adults?

Have you any worries about starting playgroup?

General observations from visit

Completed by   _____

Date   _____

Figure 5.1   The home profile Barbados Playgroup

The children all live in the local community and many of the families know each other and meet socially outside the playgroup. This makes it easier for children to settle into the playgroup when they are new to it. Nevertheless, the staff take the settling-in process very seriously. There is sometimes debate about whether observations of children should be recorded on the first day. Occasionally it is argued that this is unfair to the children, because they are adjusting to a new experience, and so won't show themselves at their best level intellectually. The argument is that staff should wait for several weeks until the child has settled before recording observations in order to be fair to the child. This is only true if recording observations is seen a way of testing a child. If, however, it is seen as important in mapping the child's journey of development and learning, then starting points, such as their first day at the playgroup, become important. They are part of the keyperson and child getting to know each other, tuning into each other, and developing a trusting relationship, so that the child feels safe and secure. At Barbados the staff prefer to describe the keyperson as the keycarer as they feel that this term is more nurturing and not so formal. It is vital for staff to reflect on the terminology they use, and to make sure that it holds meaning for them. In this chapter, because of the 'official' EYFS label 'keyperson', both will be used side by side, so as to respect the thinking of the practitioners working together at Barbados.

In the charts (Figure 5.2) below, we can see how two year old Billy's first day is carefully observed and noted by his keycarer (EYFS keyperson), Hayley (who is his grandmother). He has a good morning, finding interesting things to do, using Hayley as an anchor to return to. She is already his safe haven. He already senses that when he falls over, he will be treated kindly and helped when he attends the playgroup three days a week. He knows Hayley, as she had been part of his community and social life prior to starting at Barbados Playgroup. This helps him to tackle his first day.

A chart is filled in with the family, probably based on Sheila Wolfendale's original work, and keeping her title, 'All About Me' (Figure 5.3). The idea is to make a portrait of the child. This helps staff and family to work together with the child in what Peter Elfer and Dorothy Selleck (2012) call the Triangle of Trust. Another important feature of the Barbados Playgroup is the **Family Diary** (Figure 5.4), which is kept for a week. This is then placed in the child's folder together with the **First Day** and the **All About Me** forms. (Figures 5.2 and 5.3).

It is clear that Billy enjoys books and stories. He has a full social life visiting family, and plays with his sister Ellie-Mae very constructively. We can see that he has a very positive first day at the playgroup. The family diary, however, shows that his introductory visit (a little while prior to beginning to attend Barbados Playgroup regularly) tires him out. Very sensibly, his mother makes sure he has a quiet day following the introductory visit. There is a great deal of debate about whether children should attend every day, or only on some days, which may or may not be consecutive. The argument for daily

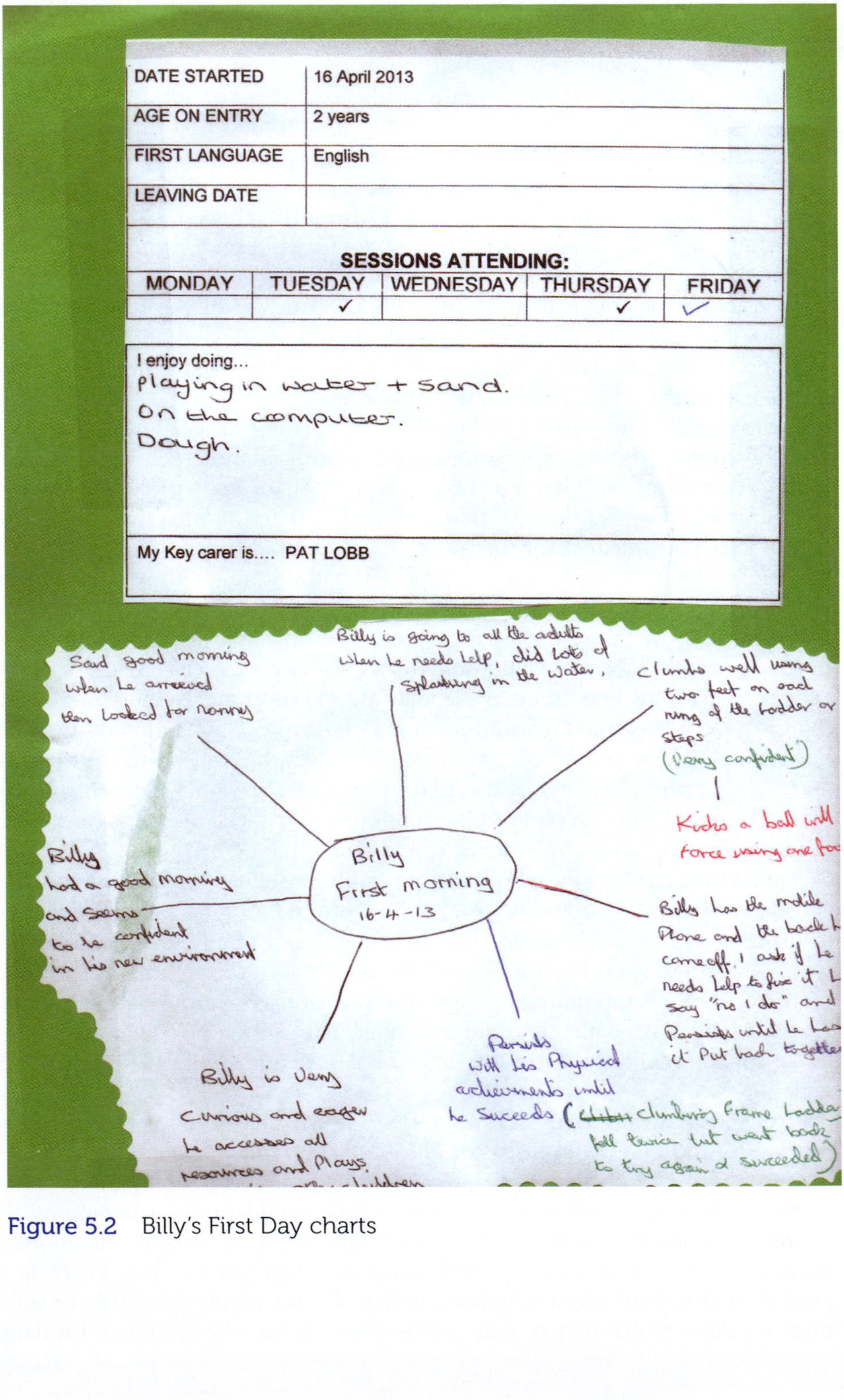

DATE STARTED	16 April 2013	
AGE ON ENTRY	2 years	
FIRST LANGUAGE	English	
LEAVING DATE		

SESSIONS ATTENDING:				
MONDAY	TUESDAY	WEDNESDAY	THURSDAY	FRIDAY
	✓		✓	✓

I enjoy doing...

Playing in water + sand.
On the computer.
Dough.

My Key carer is.... PAT LOBB

Figure 5.2   Billy's First Day charts

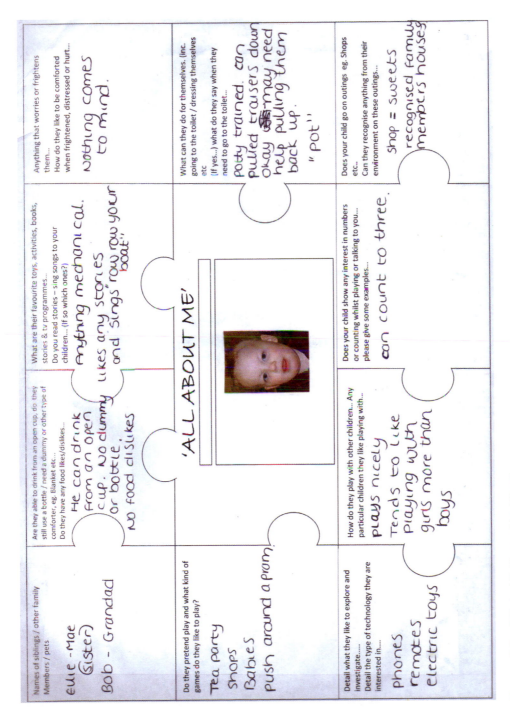

Figure 5.3   Billy's All About Me Chart

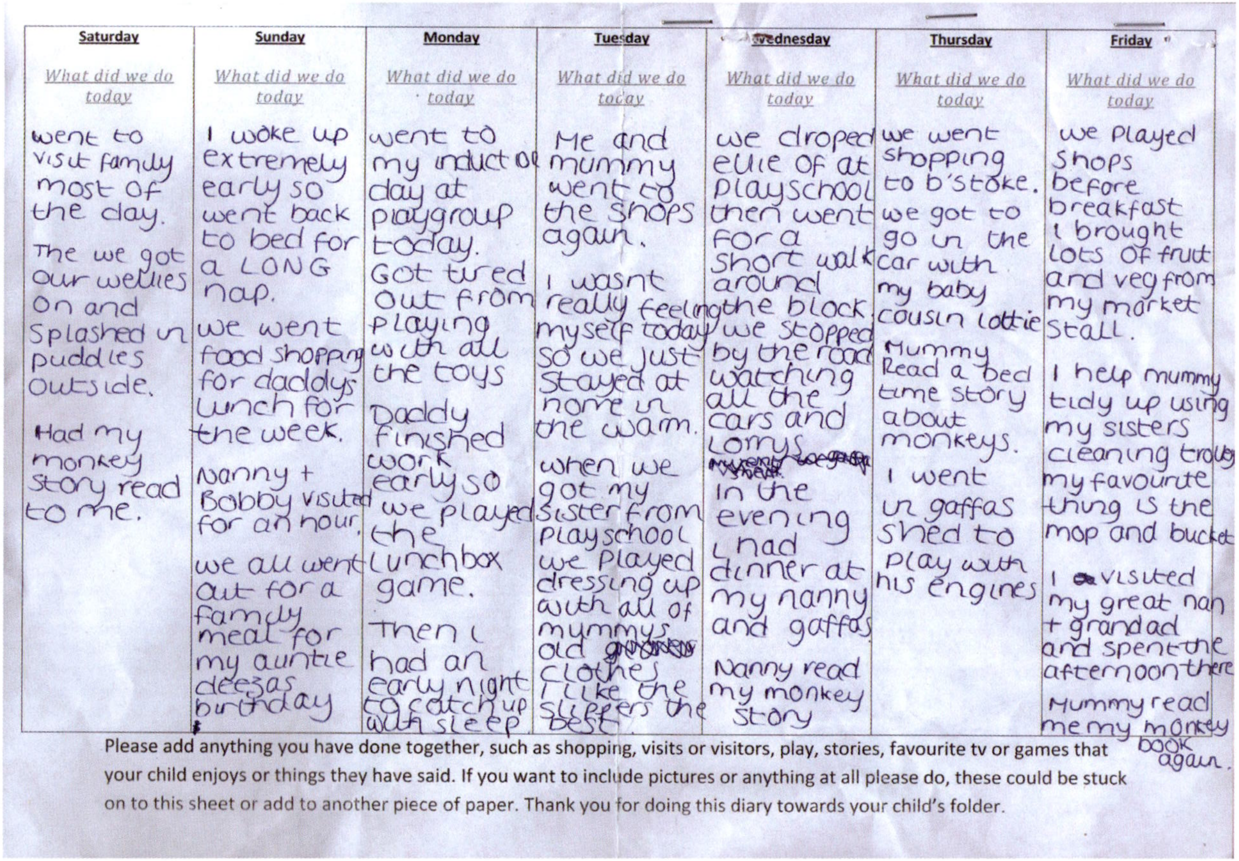

Saturday	Sunday	Monday	Tuesday	Wednesday	Thursday	Friday
What did we do today	*What did we do today*	*What did we do today*	*What did we do today*	*What did we do today*	*What did we do today*	*What did we do today*
Went to visit family most of the day. The we got our wellies on and splashed in puddles outside. Had my monkey story read to me.	I woke up extremely early so went back to bed for a LONG nap. We went food shopping with all for daddys lunch for the week. Nanny + Bobby visited for an hour. We all went out for a family meal for my auntie deesas birthday	went to my induction day at playgroup today. Got tired out from playing with all the toys Daddy finished work early so we played the lunchbox game. Then I had an early night fell asleep with sleep	Me and mummy went to the shops again. I wasnt really feeling myself today so we just stayed at home in the warm. when we got my sister from playschool we played dressing up with all of mummys old clothes I like the sisters the	we droped ellie of at playschool then went for a short walk around the block we stopped by the road watching all the cars and lorrys in the evening I had dinner at my nanny and gaffas Nanny read my monkey story	we went shopping to b'stoke. we got to go in the car with my baby cousin lottie mummy Read a bed time story about monkeys. I went in gaffas shed to play with his engines	we played shops before breakfast I brought lots of fruit and veg from my market stall. I help mummy tidy up using my sisters cleaning troll my favourite thing is the mop and bucket I visited my great nan + grandad and spent one afternoon there Mummy read me my monkey book again.

Please add anything you have done together, such as shopping, visits or visitors, play, stories, favourite tv or games that your child enjoys or things they have said. If you want to include pictures or anything at all please do, these could be stuck on to this sheet or add to another piece of paper. Thank you for doing this diary towards your child's folder.

Figure 5.4 Billy's Family Diary chart

attendance tends to be based on the idea that children need routine. The argument for less regular attendance (in Billy's case he attends Tuesdays, Thursdays and Fridays) is that two year olds can get very tired after a session, and so less intense attendance might suit children better.

We also see from the family diary that he loves his visits to Gaffa's shed to 'play with his engines'. He calls his grandfather Gaffa. Billy enjoyed 'watching all the cars and lorries'. He spends some of his weekends with Gaffa attending rallies where his grandfather exhibits his vintage engines and Billy is often found with Gaffa helping and tinkering with the engines. These observations become significant when we see what he chooses to do at the Barbados Playgroup when he attends regularly. Early on, in the 'All About Me' notes written by staff and parents together, he is shown to like mechanical things.

Once the children start at the Barbados Playgroup, staff take a very individual approach: the keycarer (EYFS keyperson) keeps further observations, and some of these are recorded, but not all. This is because, very wisely, staff discuss the learning of the children at the end of each morning. Because many of the children are two year olds, it is essential that they feel secure and have sufficient adult attention paid to their learning. This means there need to be adult:child ratios which allow this. Otherwise there would be a lack of quality of educational experience for these very young children. Because the adult:child ratios are four children to one adult for two year olds, Billy's keyperson Hayley has been able to have the kinds of conversation with him that develop his rotation schema and lead to his learning more about rotation.

Billy's rotation schema

Billy loves mechanical things and he spends time at playgroup exploring things that rotate. He learns more about rotation with Gaffa in his shed. His grandfather has vintage engines, and Billy is being introduced to these early. In the photographs in this chapter, we can see that he is developing a serious interest in how the various parts of a vehicle work together. The development of an understanding of 'cause-and-effect' is emerging, although this will develop more fully when he is older. The fuller sense of cause-and-effect is present when a child understands the beginning and end (this causes that) and also what leads from the beginning to the end of a situation.

An example would be that the child understands that the wheels need to turn round if the bike or pram is to move along the ground.

Beginning – The wheels begin to turn round

Ending – The bike or pram moves along

For a fuller sense of cause-and-effect, a child would need to understand that in order to make the bike move there need to be pedals, and also understand how the pedals are attached to the wheels, and that by pushing the pedals with the feet, the wheels are made to turn because these are linked to the pedals.

In the photograph (Figure 5.5), we can see that Billy is turning a pedal with his hands, and he can see the wheel turning. He is certainly exploring the important things about a bike and how to make it move! But we can't be sure that as well as exploring he really understands the cause-and-effect relationship between the pedals and the wheels.

Billy is certainly intensely interested in the bike. We only have to observe his body language to know this. On the Laevers and Declerq (2012) involvement scale, we would score him as deeply involved in his exploration of the bike. Spending time with Gaffa means that it is likely he is already having the kinds of conversation that are helping him to work out what causes what to happen. At the playgroup he also expands his vocabulary, because the staff are commenting very helpfully on what he does when exploring the bike. When he turns the bike upside down to turn the pedals and watch the wheels, he is not reprimanded and told to ride the bike properly. The staff – making careful observations of the children they work with – know that Billy is only going to do something like this if he needs to as part of his learning. They comment on the fact that the bike is upside down. They give him vocabulary such as 'pedal' and 'it rotates'. Two year olds take in new vocabulary at a fast rate if they are given the opportunities. This shows how staff can observe, support and extend Billy's vocabulary appropriately using schemas.

Louis et al. (2013: 41) define the rotation schemas as:

Figure 5.5   Cause-and-effect is developing: turning the pedal causes the wheels of the bike to turn

An interest in things which turn, such as knobs, taps, keys, wind-up toys. This schema can also be seen in children's actions when they run or ride bikes around in circles or spin round and round, or make circle and spiral patterns in paint or other messy play.

Billy's fascination with things that rotate can be seen throughout the morning session. It is also clear in the observations made by staff and parents that it is something sustained. Beginning to understand rotation (a schema) is a learning strategy through which his brain is developing deeper understanding. He seems to be focused on the cause-and-effect aspect as there are no observations revealing any indication of pretend play around this time. However, he will stay at Barbados Playgroup until he begins school, and there will probably also be observations showing his development of pretend play together with those of cause-and-effect. These are two of the most important aspects of developing learning in the period from toddler to seven years old or so. Understanding schemas helps adults to help children develop their learning.

Just as Billy is fascinated by the pedals on the bike, and the fact that when he turns those pedals the wheels go round, so he is interested in the pram (Figure 5.6). He turns the pram upside down. He stands and looks at the wheels. They do not turn round. Then he turns them with his hands. In some ways, this is a more challenging situation than the exploration of the bike and its pedals. When the bike was upside down, Billy could see that his action on the pedal caused the wheel to turn. This relates to what happens when the bike is the right way up. In the case of the pram, it is not so easy to see that the only way to make the wheel go round when the pram is upright is to push it with your hands on the handle of the pram. The pram is not so mechanical. It doesn't have pedals. In his play Billy is able to apply his existing knowledge about the bike and its pedals to a new situation with the pram. This shows his knowledge of a cause-and-effect relationship. This will develop, with the right help, into a functional dependency relationship, when he is able to see the initial step and how each subsequent part of the sequence – with transformations along the way – results in the final state.

Real-life situations have their place in helping children in their learning. Probably when Billy spends time with Gaffa, he sees him turn bikes and other vehicles upside down. The real bike and pram at the playgroup help him towards working out how they work mechanically. But small world toys also have a place. He loves the miniature 'Thomas the Tank Engine'

Figure 5.6   Billy with the pram

Figure 5.7   Billy with the train

that he comes across at the play-group (Figure 5.7). Vocabulary such as 'axle' will help him to understand how the wheels are linked to each other. The axle links two wheels, one on each side of the engine. There are three axles and six wheels. He won't yet understand all of this, but seeing that an axle joins wheels helps. It leads him towards understanding pistons and how they turn the axles. It is a move towards seeing why the engine needs something to make it move the pistons, which turn the axles. 'Thomas the Tank Engine' needs steam power. He is learning about this with Gaffa. The engine driver stokes the engine to heat the water, to make the steam. One thing causes another.

Billy is on the way with his grasp of cause-and-effect. The experiences he has in real-life situations relating to mechanical objects will be important in taking his understanding of cause-and -effect further. The conversations he has will also be of crucial importance, so that he increasingly articulates what is causing what to happen. Adults play a key part in giving children worthwhile experiences and talking with (not at) them.

As far as his pretend play is concerned, we can see glimmerings in the way that he enjoys imitating the actions he sees Gaffa performing on engines. Observation is key to capturing this as it develops. During the next four years, from age 3–7, if all goes well, this is likely to burgeon and flourish.

Katie-anne's trajectory and enveloping schemas

When Katie-anne made her first visit to Barbados Playgroup, she, like Billy, enjoyed it but was tired and needed a quiet afternoon afterwards. Katie-anne is two years old. The diary of her activities in the week in which she made the visit show that family times are an important feature in her life (Figure 5.8). She plays with her older brother Reece at home. She goes shopping with her mother, and is taken to the park to feed the ducks. She visits her grandparents.

Saturday	Sunday	Monday	Tuesday	Wednesday	Thursday	Friday
What did we do today	*What did we do today*	*What did we do today*	*What did we do today*	*What did we do today*	*What did we do today*	*What did we do today*
We went food shopping with my Brother and Daddy and then went home and done lot's of playing and then watch my Favourite TV Show in the night garden.	I Spent Day at home Playing with my Big Brother Reece and help mum tidy my room	today is my Birthday I open my Preset and took my Brother to School and then went to Spend my Birthday money and then feed Ducks. And then went to McDo for my tea and then my Nanny and Grandad Came around.	I play with all my new toys and Watch T.V. In the night Jaren, Mickey mouse and walk to get my Big Brother from School.	my first Day at School and I lovly It gave home and had lunch and had little rest and Carry on Playing	wish I School today But Stay at home Play and Saw my Nanny Grandad.	School today and I had great fun Come home had lunch Playing got my Brother School. watch T.V

Please add anything you have done together, such as shopping, visits or visitors, play, stories, favourite tv or games that your child enjoys or things they have said. If you want to include pictures or anything at all please do, these could be stuck on to this sheet or add to another piece of paper. Thank you for doing this diary towards your child's folder.

Figure 5.8 Family Diary for the week Katie-anne makes her first visit to the playgroup

Feeding the ducks is enjoyable for her, and as the observations begin to show, this might be because they have trajectory appeal. Throwing bread to the ducks involves trajectories, and tracing parabolas in the air with the bread. The trajectory schema is an important one, and is often observed when children show a fascination for throwing objects. Some throwing is unacceptable, but feeding the ducks is. When children have opportunities such as this, they are less likely to throw objects in ways that will cause danger to others, or annoy adults because they make things untidy. In this example, throwing begins during the toddler period as joyful movement linked to the senses – feeling the crumbly bread, looking, hearing the ducks quacking and splashing through the water to reach the bread, tasting the air, and smelling the river (what the poet Rupert Brooke calls the 'unforgettable, unforgotten river smell'). Gradually the young child, Katie-anne in this instance, begins to understand that throwing the bread in a particular way means it reaches a particular duck. Throwing, and the trajectory traced by the bread, become more refined and combined through exploratory play. The trajectory is aimed at a target, namely the duck who wants to eat the bread.

The parents and staff will use the 'All About Me' chart (Figure 5.9) to help them settle in Katie-anne at the playgroup. It chimes with the Family Diary. It is important that staff note anything that might frighten or make Katie-anne anxious. At home she has a dog, but her parents want the staff to be aware that black cats distress her. However it is also crucial that they know how to comfort her if a black cat should come into the outdoor area of the hall where the playgroup is based. If this were to happen, she would need a cuddle. Karen, as the keycarer (EYFS keyperson), will be alert to this possibility. You never know when a black cat might turn up in the garden!

The settling-in period at Barbados Playgroup goes well for Katie-anne (Figures 5.10 and 5.11). She attends each morning. She is observed painting, using glue, filling and emptying containers, and playing with the dolls. It takes a few weeks to piece together the observations so that they make sense. Of course, adults don't have to understand everything that involves children's development and learning. That would be impossible. But if they are going to work with other people's children then it helps if they find out some of the significant aspects of the learning, so that as staff they can help a child such as Katie-anne to get the most out of her time at playgroup.

The observation that she enjoys putting things in her bag proves to be a significant one. Enveloping objects in a bag is a classic sign of an envelopment schema. She seems to have a strong envelopment schema. At home she climbed into the laundry basket, and wanted the lid put over her (Figure 5.12). Two year olds often demonstrate their schemas with their whole body. She certainly does enjoy putting small objects into a bag, but she also seeks out a situation where she can put the whole of herself inside something which completely envelops her. Staff observe the effects of the envelopment schema as Katie-anne begins to modify her ideas in different situations.

Names of siblings / other family Members / pets	Are they able to drink from an open cup, do they still use a bottle / need a [dummy] or other type of comforter, eg. Blanket etc... Do they have any food likes/dislikes...	What are their favourite toys, activities, books, stories & tv programmes... Do you read stories – sing songs to your children... (If so which ones?)	Anything that worries or frightens them... How do they like to be comforted when frightened, distressed or hurt...
Reece (brother 5y) Nemo – Dog. Budgies- Joey / Lou 3 fish -	open cup. eats anything	Dolls. Pushing/Pulling Night Garden. Mickey mouse club house. filling/emptying.	Black cats. Cuddles.

'ALL ABOUT ME'

Do they pretend play and what kind of games do they like to play?		What can they do for themselves. (inc. going to the toilet / dressing themselves etc (If yes...) what do they say when they need to go to the toilet...
Pretends to cook- Push baby in pram.		toilet training. Brush her teeth. helps with clothes

Speech & Language skills (eg what can your child say? Can they follow instructions?)	How do they play with other children... Any particular children they like playing with... Can/does your child share...	Does your child show any interest in numbers or counting whilst playing or talking to you... Do they like to explore and investigate... If so please give some examples...	Does your child go on outings. eg. Shops etc... Can they recognise anything from their environment on these outings...
uses gesture. Single words. follows instructions.	likes to play with her brother, neighbours.	Copies cute adults etc counting. loves to explore + investigate - likes to help with chores.	Shops- nannans – park- Reece's school- walk the dog.

Figure 5.9   Katie-anne's All About Me chart

Figure 5.10   Katie-anne's settling in chart

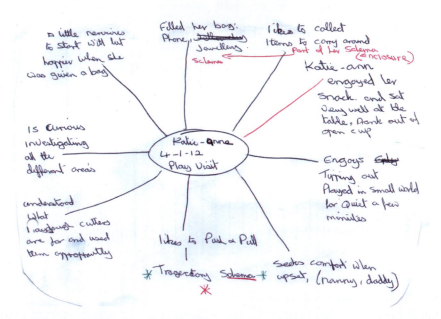

Figure 5.11   Katie-anne's First Day chart

In the outdoor area she likes to smear mud and cover things (Figure 5.13). She enjoys doing the same with paint. Covering things over is a sign of envelopment. She is using her schema through her senses and movements. The feel of the mud and the look of the covering over process are beckoning her. It is perhaps also noteworthy that she has chosen to wear dressing-up clothes (a regular thing) which cover her as the dress is long. Envelopment is a strong schema for Katie-anne. Envelopment often re-emerges with strength when in a new situation. It is what Chris Athey, who pioneered the educational application of schemas, described as an old and comfortable schema. The foetus enveloped in the womb is an early form of this, and now Katie-anne chooses to be enveloped in the dressing-up clothes as she settles into and feels confident in the play-group.

Perhaps the fact that the enveloping schema has come to the surface empowers Katie-anne to explore her trajectory schema with gusto and energy. Gibson writes about 'affordances'. Things in our physical and peopled environment cause earlier schemas to surface. It shows that we can use our earlier learning as a resource to deal with new situations (i.e. starting playgroup for Katie-Anne).

Two year olds often puzzle – and at time annoy – adults with their habit of wrapping rope or string around furniture. But doing this seems to be important to them! Katie-anne wraps rope around a trolley, but when we see her expression of deep concentration, this alerts us that what she is doing is fascinating her (Figure 5.14). The challenge for us is establishing

Figure 5.12   Katie-anne's envelopment schema: she has enveloped her whole body with the laundry basket

Figure 5.13   Covering objects with mud: envelopment schema

Figure 5.14   Exploring a trajectory made of rope, but what is Katie-anne trying to learn? How can we help her?

what it is that she is trying to learn about. How can we help to embed and extend her thinking?

Once again, we are seeing the deep involvement that Ferre Laevers describes as being at the centre of children's learning. Observing Katie-anne here alerts us that we must take seriously what she is doing. She seems to have an idea that she needs to pull on the rope the trajectory makes. She also seems to know that the rope should be attached to something. In the next photo (Figure 5.15) we can see that she looks quietly pleased. The trajectory rope is attached to the box, and she can pull this along. Here is the beginning of an understanding of cause-and-effect, developing from the sensual and movement elements of her trajectory schema. Gradually she will begin to be able to identify the beginning, the end, and what needs to happen in between in order to gain a deeper understanding of cause-and-effect.

Chris Athey (1990) called this deeper understanding of cause-and-effect the 'functional dependency' of a schema. This means the rope that is pulled is

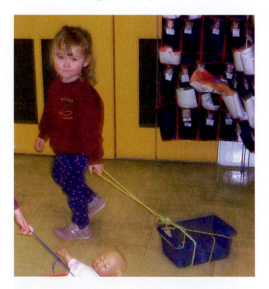

Figure 5.15   Katie-anne is beginning to understand the cause-and-effect relationship between the trajectory rope and pulling the box along

attached by a knot, and wrapped around the box, so that it can be pulled along. Two year olds are famous for their love of pull-along toys. But seven year olds are equally famous for their love of how to tie things together – knots and bows feature in their lives. Selecting a reef knot or slip knot and avoiding a granny knot (which is nearly impossible to undo once tied and pulled on) is important to these older children. All of this shows the journey a child makes in developing the cause-and-effect aspect of a trajectory schema. The trajectory schema shows in many forms, but throwing bread to ducks in the park and pull-along situations give two examples of the important learning that two year olds are in the middle of. Respecting that learning is crucial, as it can easily be stamped out or constrained if it is not encouraged at this time in a child's learning.

Why work in this way?

It is always a good idea to link with the past to see what seemed to work well, and to decide how to take best practice into a new age and generation. This does not mean handing down good practice in an unchanged form. But it does mean identifying the essence of good practice such that it is not necessary to reinvent the wheel with each generation of practitioners. It is more efficient to build on, extend and expand what has gone before, and then to adjust, modify and change those aspects that need changing.

In this chapter, we can see the importance of working closely with the parents and families of young children. We can also see the value of observation that is informed. The staff at Barbados Playgroup are working hard to learn about theory and research which they can apply in their practice. Schemas have illuminated their observations of the children at play as they are learning. There is a bit of a chicken-and-an-egg situation here! The traditional practice of observation comes first. Learning how to observe is key to good practice. But practitioners can't observe in a vacuum. The observation needs to be informed. Knowing about schemas gives practitioners a framework through which to interpret their observations. But of course, it would be wrong only to use schemas to interpret a child's learning. There are other frameworks of theory and other research which can help practitioners. The key thing is to have a mixture of theory and research which does not lead to contradictory practices. That would confuse both the staff and children.

The study and use of schemas in developing the learning of young children grew out of Piagetian theory, but have moved forward since then (Nutbrown, 2011; Bruce, 2011a,b,c; Roberts, 2009; Matthews, 2003; Arnold, 2003; Atherton and Nutbrown, 2013; Louis, 2013) to take account of more recent theory and research, or to explore links to other theories. It is always most helpful when theories and research are applicable in accessible ways for practitioners to make use of. Schemas are of this kind, and are now widely used in practice, both in the UK and internationally. They are found in the UK Government framework documents (Curriculum Guidance for the Foundation Stage 2000, Birth to Three Matters 2002 and Early Years Foundation Stage 2012).

It is important not to discard what has gone before. Each generation of practitioners needs to look at what has led practice in previous times, so that lessons can be learned from the past. It is then that we will find treasure! And treasure becomes a resource. The staff at Barbados use as a resource and treasure the legacy of the Playgroup Movement. They emphasise play and the community experience of children coming together to play in a group.

Each generation finds its own vocabulary to explain and describe what it does and how it works. This is where practitioners need to link with theory and research.

It is important for practitioners to learn and use (in their own way) the vocabulary of government framework documents. Otherwise there will be difficulty when inspectors (for example, known in England as Ofsted; in Scotland as HMIe and Care) use official terms, and practitioners are not bilingual. Practitioners need to understand that inspectors will not be bilingual. They are trained to use and look for officially framed, articulated and described good practice. Practitioners need to be bilingual in order to demonstrate their good practice.

One of the reasons that practitioners continue to use their own language through which to observe children, and to note, follow and help them to learn, is that they understand this and so can develop their practice. Schemas give a clear framework and vocabulary which practitioners can use with each other and with parents to describe how children are learning. They make sense. Official documents keep changing, and the terminology shifts with them. They are often written by people who have never worked with young children. But, in the main, inspectors will not be able to reach out and use both theoretical and research-based language and official language. Thus it falls to practitioners to do that.

What we have learned

- Use the past and find what is treasure – such as the importance of **informed observation** that helps practitioners and parents to plan together.
- Use the past as a resource but also recognise the need to use **current theory and research** to make this a meaningful process. Knowing about schemas helps the practitioners of today to observe children and gives vocabulary which is easy to understand in today's context.
- Sharing observations between staff is important, and a daily discussion is helpful. Practitioners need time for this. Half-day sessions in settings allow this to be possible.
- Identifying what interests children, and working with this, will help practitioners to go deeper with a child's learning, but also has the wonderful effect of broadening that child's learning.
- It is vital not to under-estimate what children can learn. When practitioners study and use theory and research relating to schemas they can help children (two year olds in this chapter) to see cause-and-effect relationships, and enter the work of pretend with more depth.
- Play matters. Two year olds benefit from having plenty of choice. They then find what interests them, and they learn better if they develop their own educationally worthwhile interests. The group time at the end of the morning can then be relaxed and informal, as children of this age are tired by then, and need to be calm at that time.
- Finding efficient ways to capture the journey of learning that each child makes is of central importance. Starting points and the journey itself need to be recorded, but it is the significant markers that illuminate the development of learning in the child.

Reflective question

- How can you develop and improve the way in which you act on the observations you make of children in a variety of learning situations? Work on two ways in which you can support and extend children at play. You might, for example, identify the child's schema and use that to inform your planning. You could also read more about schemas so that you create a backcloth for your practical work with children.

Further reading

Atherton, F. and Nutbrown, C. (2103) *Understanding Schemas and Young Children: From Birth to Three*. London: Sage.

Louis, S. (2013) *Schemas: Characteristics of Effective Learning*. London: BAECE/ Early Education. Available at www.earlyeducation.org.uk

Louis, S., Beswick, C., Magraw, L. and Hayes, L. (Edited by Sally Featherstone) (2008) *Again! Again! Understanding Schemas in Young Children*. London: A&C Black.

Louis, S. (2012) *Schemas*. Southwark Council; In the Picture.

Nutbrown, C. (2011) *Threads of Thinking: Schemas and Young Children's Learning* (4th edn). London: Sage.

Ouvry, M. (2003) *Exercising Muscles and Minds: Outdoor Play and the Early Years Curriculum*, London: National Early Years Network.

CHAPTER 6

WORKING WITH CHILDREN WITH AUTISM

In this chapter you will learn about:

- How to take an inclusive approach to working with children with autism.
- The importance of observing small steps in a child's learning which are significant markers in that child.

The setting

Eastwood is a maintained Nursery School and Children's Centre with a history of excellence confirmed by every Ofsted inspection since it was founded in the 1970s. This chapter celebrates the sustained quality of its work with children and their families up until the recent retirement of Liz Rook, the Director. It is significant that the University of Roehampton has awarded her an honorary degree to mark the occasion. The university has been closely linked with Eastwood. The beautiful Froebel College grounds in the university are used for the Forest School, and research is regularly undertaken by university staff at Eastwood, sometimes supported by Froebel Trust funding.

Since its foundation in the 1970s, Eastwood has always welcomed children with special educational needs and disabilities. It now includes several children each year – referred from various parts of the Local Authority – who have autism (ASD).

In the chapter on schemas we saw how vital it is for early childhood practitioners to be 'bilingual': when working with children with disabilities and Special Educational Needs (SEN) these practitioners need to become multilingual. However, there is a 'home' language, and that is the time-honoured vocabulary of early childhood education used across the world (e.g. at EECERA Conferences), informed by theory and research that are updated continually. This can be utilised to great effect and success as a navigational tool to guide practitioners through the requirements of the official documents or specialist medical and therapist approaches. In this chapter, we will find that practitioners need to be comfortable in three 'languages':

- **The time-honoured early childhood practice language** and approach to practice (based on relevant theory and research) informed by current theory and research.
- **The language of official framework documents**, often legally required, according to country (e.g. EYFS in England, Curriculum for Excellence in Scotland).
- **Medical language** and an approach to working with children with disabilities and special educational needs used by therapists (e.g. speech and language, physiotherapy, occupational therapists, etc.).

But – and this is a big 'but' – every language has its culture. It is important that the three approaches do not clash and do battle with each other. That uses energy in unhelpful ways.

The first and most crucial thing is that the official framework documents (often legally enshrined) must not be used as the starting point for practice. Practitioners need to apply their knowledge of early childhood practice arising from time-honoured practice that is tried and tested.

Governments change, and official documents change with them. Official documents even change if, within one government administration, the minister changes. If, by contrast, time-honoured practice which has stood the test of time is the basis, and informed, adjusted, modified and illuminated through current theory and research, then practitioners have the navigational tools they need to help them find their way through any official document in any country in ways which promote quality.

If this generalist approach to early childhood principles and practice is applied, it makes it easier for specialists to make their contribution. But the early childhood practitioner needs to learn the specialists' (often medical) terminology if this is to be possible.

Phrases like 'restricted and repetitive interests' are used in the medical approach, and can cause difficulty when, for example, speech and language therapists work with early childhood teachers and nursery practitioners. A phrase like this may well seem very negative, or very narrow, and early childhood practitioners may prefer to describe a child as having a specialist and focused interest in something. Medical terms can sound very judgemental to a generalist trained early childhood practitioner. In Chapter 3 we saw the necessity of including parents in these discussions.

It is of deep importance that practitioners trained within different backgrounds should work together in ways which are constructive, positive, and respect each other's training. Discussion together helps. So does sharing an observation. Looking together at the different observations taken of the child by the staff can prove very helpful. A variety of perspectives can be discussed and teased out.

Reflection on the phrase 'restricted and repetitive interest' is a good start. When a generalist practitioner observes a deep interest in a child, it is something to celebrate. Three year old Tom spent a happy and intensely focused afternoon making birds out of plasticine. He made a blackbird with a yellow beak, wings and claws that meant he could balance on a tree. He made a robin which was brown, with a red breast. He made a snowy owl which he had seen at the zoo, which was white with large eyes and small ears. His parents kept the models until they fell apart. They were thrilled. Tom was able to describe the birds, and showed them to Grandma with pride. He demonstrated to her how they sat in a tree, or flew in the day or night. He sang the song:

> Little Robin Redbreast sat upon a rail
>
> Niddle, noddle went his head
>
> And waggle went his tail
>
> As Little Robin Redbreast sat upon a rail

But this example of Tom, who is building and developing a focused interest, would not be viewed as a 'restricted and repetitive interest' by a specialist in ASD. Only if Tom tackled the same activity in the same way each time, simply copying the three characters from a favourite book in which he has a 'restricted and repetitive interest', would it be described in this way.

At Eastwood there is no desire to extinguish a child's narrowly focused interest (how a generalist early childhood practitioner might describe it) or a 'restricted and repetitive interest' (how a speech and language therapist might describe it). Indeed, it would probably be impossible to do so. However, there is a great need to help the child with ASD to self regulate, and to interact with other children socially. This means that the development of joint attention is of great importance. Because the speech and language therapist is trained in 'communication' this will be a major emphasis in approaching the work with such a child.

One of the challenges for children with ASD is their difficulty in developing joint attention and in making the journey into symbolic representation. They tend to think literally, and find pretend play hard.

How the staff work: generalist early childhood practitioners and specialist therapists

At Eastwood there is a carefully thought-through framework of documents which guide both the generalist and the specialist practitioners through their

EASTWOOD ASD PROVISION		
Time	Nursery Routine	Additional ASD Activity
9.15–9.30	Welcome/Inside Play	Anchor Group – Maple Class
9.30–9.45	Key Group Time	Anchor Group – Beech
9.45–10.15	Free-Flow Play and focused activities (inc. Forest School and Jabadao)	Discovery Zone Sessions
10.15–10.45		Main nursery routine with additional support and classroom planning from ASD teacher e.g. – In class support to work on IEP targets/ access to the curriculum/peer interactions – 1-1 SLT and OT Sessions – Language Groups – Music Therapy sessions
10.45–11.15		Daily Structured Group Activities: Mon: Sensory Food Play Tues: Snack Time Wed: Snack Time Thurs: Forest School Fri: Sensory Food Group
11.15–11.30		Main nursery routine
11.30–11.45	Carpet Time with Differentiation	
11.45–12.15	1st Lunch Sitting	Outside Play
12.15	*Am/Pm Sessions swap over***	
12.15–12.45	2nd Lunch Sitting	Outside Play
12.45–13.00	Welcome/Inside Play	
13.00–13.15	Key Group Time	Anchor Group – Beech Class
13.15–13.30	Free-Flow Play and focused activities (inc. Forest School and Jabadao)	Discovery Zone Sessions
13.30–14.30		Main nursery routine with additional support and classroom planning from ASD teacher e.g. – In class support to work on IEP targets/ access to the curriculum/peer interactions – 1-1 SLT and OT Sessions – Language Groups – Music Therapy sessions
14.30–14.50		Daily Structured Group Activities: Mon: Sensory Food Play Tues: Snack Time Wed: Snack Time Thurs: Forest School Fri: Sensory Food Group
14.50–15.00		Main nursery routine
15.00–15.15	Carpet Time with Differentiation	

Figure 6.1 Eastwood ASD Provision Routine

** Children within the ASD provision either have five long morning sessions, or five long afternoon sessions. This suits most children better than having four half day sessions with one full day, which is what mainstream children at Eastwood are offered.

work with the children with ASD both on a daily basis and in the longer term. In this section of the chapter we shall explore how this works.

The children with ASD attending Eastwood are given plenty of opportunities for freely chosen play (or free flow play: Bruce, 1991; 2011b) during the day. They are also given support and guidance in socialising and joint attention with other children and the specialist practitioners in 'anchor groups'.

Although there is a general timetable with individual routines put together for individual children with ASD (see Figure 6.1), it is vital that the timetable is maintained to give children the structure and predictable routine that they need in order to be well regulated and available for learning.

However this timetable is a key part of the record-keeping and helps practitioners to plan for individual children attending Eastwood who have ASD. Some children will attend all the additional activities, such as the anchor group. Others will not. Instead they will have individual sessions with the specialist staff, but they will also spend time in the main nursery where they will experience the Eastwood nursery routines and begin to self regulate in this social environment.

In the morning, the children at Eastwood begin the day in their keyperson groups. The children with autism are usually placed in an **anchor group** in each classroom. They come together with the practitioner, who is usually the speech and language therapist, or the specialist ASD practitioner (teacher or nursery practitioner) who works with them. The aim of the anchor group is to help the children develop joint attention.

The structuring of the anchor group is influenced by the 'Little Group' training model developed in 2009 and offered by Judy Gilham, then Deputy Head, and who subsequently became Head. The 'little group' approach was devised by Gina Davies in 2009 when she was Head of the Little Group Nursery. Judy Gilham is now continuing the training programme in the nursery which is part of Eagle House.

When the children in the anchor group at Eastwood have developed sufficient language and joint attention skills to manage, they return to their own keyperson group.

Record-keeping in planning the daily anchor group

Careful record-keeping takes place. This ensures that the atmosphere, way of working and setting up of resources are right for the anchor group to gain the most from it.

The guidance notes written by the speech and language therapist make it clear that sharing an experience means that a relationship begins to be formed. Unless we can share attention, the guidance notes for staff at Eastwood say, 'we have no framework for interaction with others'. This principle underpins all of their practice with the anchor group.

Children with autism (ASD) are helped to work with and through their strengths. This adheres to the Froebelian principle that good education begins where the learner is, not where that learner 'ought' to be. It identifies a child's strengths as the starting point for teaching (not their weaknesses). Children with ASD are strong in understanding structure and in things that are visual.

The children begin to sit and attend in a social way because they find what is being presented in the anchor group interesting. It catches their attention. Gradually, as their attention grows, words can be introduced, and social interaction can be encouraged. But at first the activities need to be very visual, and to appeal emotionally by being interesting.

In the anchor group practitioners will need to plan:

- a quiet, screened off area of the room, where two practitioners work together, with one leading and the other supporting;
- a symbol on each child's visual timetable showing the anchor group: children are shown the visual timetable and the anchor group symbol and taken to the anchor group when they arrive;
- a 'now' board and a 'next' board: the children are shown that the symbol of the anchor group is now on the board, and that next on the board is the symbol for the Discovery Zone;
- a song for the anchor group to begin with: this is less challenging than using speech because it accesses the other side of the brain; the song might be about what is in the box, and is used as a repeat chorus between each activity;
- a box of activities: examples of small activities would be bubbles or spinners, while big activities would be cornflour shakers, a watering-can shower, dry ingredient cooking, tin foil, a plastic tube with water, food colour and glitter, paint splashing, ice cube bags, flour castles. The object(s) or material(s) are taken from the box with a clear beginning, middle and end;
- a box for finished-with items that are used when the activity has ended: the two boxes must be used for their purpose only, or the children will be confused; it is important that the children are not given the boxes as this will damage the novelty of the activity, and in the same way, they will become bored if they are given the objects to hold; the focus in an anchor group is to share attention or the experience;
- that each activity is repeated two or three times, so that children have the possibility of getting used to it;
- that chairs are arranged in a horseshoe, with one for each child (two to six children).

Record-keeping is essential if children are to make progress in the anchor group, for the aim is for them to join their 'keyperson group' in the main room. Records need to trace where children are in this journey, such as where they engage with simple activities like bubbles or spinners. If they begin to be able to self regulate and attend for the whole session (10 minutes) they will be ready to try something 'bigger'. It is something to celebrate when they start to be able to use the activities that have been offered to them in the anchor group (to pretend to build a sandcastle, for example). A song is used to accompany this, with each child taking a turn. Gradually, children begin to engage with pretend play using small world resources.

The **significant markers** to observe and record in anchor groups are:

- the beginning of the journey, when children need small activities, with no words, but which are visual and emotionally interesting;
- when they can self regulate through a session of 10 minutes and engage in joint attention with some language introduced with a bigger activity;
- when they can pretend to act out a bigger activity;
- when they can pretend through using small-world resources.

All full-time children with ASD who attend anchor group attend two sessions a day. Some would have benefitted from it taking place more often but this was not possible within the Eastwood routine.

The Discovery Zone

Another additional activity for children with ASD at Eastwood is the Discovery Zone. For children who find it overwhelming to be in the busy classroom for long, time spent in the sensory room, ball pool or soft play room is invaluable. These offer sensory experiences to meet their sensory needs through an individual sensory diet established by a specialist occupational therapist. They have opportunities for interaction with other children.

Jabadao and Forest School

Some of the children with ASD are able to take part with the mainstream children in the Developmental Movement sessions (Jabadao). Several members of the generalist staff have been trained in this approach (developed by the pioneer Penny Greenland, MBE), and it is a well-established part of the practice at Eastwood. There are always two members of staff working with the children.

The Forest School is another aspect of the work at Eastwood which is well embedded. The children visit the grounds of the Froebel College, which is part of the University of Roehampton, when they begin to participate in Forest School. Later they visit Richmond Park. They need to be able to walk to both of these locations. Parents are welcome to join them.

Observations are made in the usual way during Jabadao sessions, or during Forest School. It is important to see how children with ASD respond to these experiences, and also to see them in a variety of situations. For this reason, in order to capture the whole child, staff who are mainstream plan with the staff specialising in work with children with ASD. This applies to both the daily planning and the weekly planning process. Note that we need to be careful not to label children as 'ASD children'. They are children first and foremost, and so it is important to describe them as **children** – with ASD.

Children are individuals. At Eastwood all the children are educated as individuals. At the beginning of the chapter, the main framework timetable was given, showing the organisation of the day for children in the mainstream and in general terms presenting an outline structure for the children with ASD. In the next section, the individual timetables of two children with ASD are shown. The first child is preverbal and attends for the morning sessions (Figure 6.2). The second child is verbal, and attends full time.

9.15–9.30	Anchor Group
9.30–9.45	Sensory-Motor Play in classroom (water/sand)
9.45–10.15	Discovery Zone session (inc. 1-1 PECS input SLT)
10.15–10.45	Main nursery routine with support to – Access curriculum – Work on IEP targets – Develop interactions with peers and adults within child-led play – 1-1 sessions with OT/SLT as appropriate
10.45–11.15	Mon/Fri: Sensory Food Play Thurs: Differentiated Forest School Tues/Wed: as above (10.15–10.45)
11.15–11.30	Main Nursery Routine with support
11.30–11.45	TEACCH at worktable in classroom (Music Therapy once a week)
11.45 – 12.15	Outside Play

Figure 6.2   This timetable supports the development and learning of a boy who is preverbal and whose age is three years. He attends the morning session

In the next section of the chapter we shall examine what is meant by preverbal and verbal, and the different levels of communication, as well as social development in relation to children with ASD. Before doing so it will be useful to look at the timetable for a verbal child (Figure 6.3).

9.15–9.30	Free Play/Settle
9.30–9.45	Key group time
9.45–10.45	Main nursery routine with support to – Access curriculum – Work on IEP targets – Develop interactions with peers and adults within child-led play PLUS 1-1 speech session with SLT (once a week) Fine Motor Skills input from OT (once a week)
10.45–11.15	Tues/Wed: Snack time (act as model and develop spoken language opportunities)
11.15–11.30	Main Nursery Routine with support
11.30–11.45	Mainstream Carpet Time
11.45–12.45	Outside Play and Lunch
12.45–13.00	Free Play/Settle
13.00–13.15	Key Group Time
13.15–15.00	Main Nursery Routine with support to – Access curriculum – Work on IEP targets – Develop interactions with peers and adults within child-led play PLUS Language Group with SLT (once a week)
15.00–15.15	Carpet Time

Figure 6.3   This timetable supports the development and learning of a boy who is verbal and whose age is four years. He attends full time

Using observation to assess the communication stage of a child with ASD

Most children learn to speak naturally, and the challenge then is to ensure that they spend time with people who are fluent in the language, and who engage with them during worthwhile educational experiences, having interesting conversations together. There is concern that many children are developing language too slowly and with narrow vocabularies, and this has resulted in excellent frameworks such as *Communication Matters* (DfES, 2005) and *Every Child a Talker* (DCFS, 2008–10). But for children with ASD the development of language is a challenge, and it will not take place 'typically', although many children with ASD develop some spoken language without any intervention. It does not just depend on making sure the child spends time with people who can provide a rich language and physical environment. A child with ASD might spend a great deal of time in an ideal language provision, but may not acquire language without informed support from those who know about and are trained in working with children who have ASD. However, there is a huge range of language (and all other) abilities across children on the Autistic Spectrum and there is a whole group of children (previously called 'Asperger's') who achieve age appropriate language but experience difficulties in how to use that language appropriately within social interactions. There are also those who may never achieve spoken language but will learn to communicate in other ways (i.e. through symbols).

This is not to say that mainstream documents are not useful to all practitioners working with children with ASD. The English document 'Characteristics of Learning' by Helen Moylett and Nancy Stewart (2013) is greatly valued by both the speech and language therapist team and the mainstream staff at Eastwood. But there is a need for more precise assessment for children with ASD, because language, communication, social and symbolic development do not take place naturally.

The first thing is to establish where the child is in terms of the different aspects of their communication. There was a useful statement from John Holt in the 1960s which said that in order to find a man who is lost in a wood, you need to know where he is. The speech and language therapist at Eastwood has found the SCERTS Model takes a holistic approach, which chimes well with the time-honoured early childhood education traditions as well as the EYFS (the English legally enshrined framework for working in early childhood education and care).

In establishing the support needs of the two boys whose timetables we have looked at, we need to see if and how they use words or symbols to communicate, and how often they do so. We also need to observe whether they can show that they understand by using objects, people or activities to do so. It is important to establish if the child seems to intend any communication.

The first little boy, who is preverbal, is at the stage when he needs the practitioner to use the 'Social Partner' section of the assessment in order to develop informed plans for developing his learning. This helps to work out how developed he is in terms of 'joint attention'. We need to know if he simply responds when we communicate with him, or whether he initiates his interacting with us. Observation will also tell us how much he uses eye contact, and follows people or objects with his eyes, and is engaged and involved with the session.

It is important to use observation to see how much he reads facial expressions, interpreting them and imitating them from others during interactions. Children and adults do this naturally when communicating with each other, but children with ASD do not.

In the same way, seeking comfort, or wanting to play a game, greeting someone, or calling to them, taking turns and showing off, are all **significant markers** in the journey towards 'social communication'. Another notable aspect of social communication is whether a child comments on situations or an object. If communication breaks down, it is important to observe whether they can repeat or repair by modifying what they say in order to improve the communication with someone, however they communicate.

'Joint attention' and using words are both crucial in the early stages of 'social communication', but observation of the development of self regulation is too. This involves observing how the child explores the environment, if the child becomes overwhelmed or manages to leave situations when they are too exciting. The fluency of their observations captures social competence (i.e. understanding of self and others). How the child shows emotion, and what the response is when someone tries to soothe and offer help, are also key observations to record.

The therapist staff specialising in ASD need to use these observations to inform their planning with their generalist colleagues and within the specialist team. In this way, the little boy who is preverbal can be supported by appropriate teaching.

The same applies to the little boy who is four years old and verbal. There are other sections of the SCERTS Model which are relevant to his educational needs. These are the 'Language Partner' and the 'Conversational Partner' sections. These give more detail than would be needed for most children in encouraging language development.

Sharing observations and planning with the parents

Throughout this book great emphasis has been placed on sharing observations with parents, and inviting them into the planning that is informed by the observations. Parents receive home visits as part of this. Every year, at Eastwood, there is also an end of the year review group when the parents whose children have ASD are invited to a discussion with governors who have a particular interest in ASD. Parents dislike the use of jargon. But they find examples of what the children do very helpful in discussion. The support they receive is invaluable as they face the challenges of bringing up their children. Talking with other parents who understand some of the difficulties they experience, or with parents who are more experienced than they are, is very helpful.

The observations made and recorded by staff help inform planning of the education of the children with ASD, but they also serve another vital purpose. They help parents to gain insight into their child, to appreciate their learning, and to see progress. The hardest thing for parents is to feel their child is not making progress. Good observation shows small changes which over time will demonstrate a child's learning journey. This will be deeply helpful. Parents of children with ASD often report that one of the hardest things for them is looking for progress when there seems to be none. But being supported in observing, with the staff, the detail and significant markers showing progress is reassuring and comforting. It helps.

What we have learned

In this chapter, we have explored how it is possible to have an inclusive approach to working with children with ASD. The challenges are not insignificant, but they are very worthwhile and produce quality of practice when observation is at the heart of the work, together with insights from practitioners trained in child development and education.

Records need to be as follows:

- User-friendly, efficient and effective in the use of time they demand. Record-keeping should not drain staff energy.
- Jargon free, or if jargon is needed it should be translated from specialist terminology into generalist early childhood education terms so that it is understood by all of the staff and parents.
- It is important for the expertise of all the staff to inform and feed into the record-keeping and planning, and so joint staff meetings, daily and weekly, are vital.
- Parents should be included in ways that are right for them. This may be through home visits, group meetings when parents get together and discuss with staff, daily touch-base feedback with the keyperson, or through the child's written profile being regularly shared with the parent(s).
- Accessible enough for parents to engage with, with observations showing practical examples of their child's learning using photography.
- Records need to show starting points (a baseline) and the journey of learning. For children with ASD the detail of the journey is key in giving significant markers that can be acted on in educationally important ways.
- There should be a joined-up record-keeping system, not a fragmented one with specialists working separate from the generalist early childhood education staff, such as the keyperson.

Reflections on this chapter

- It is essential to develop a system of record-keeping which is holistic and seamless, but which is also inclusive such that children with ASD will have records giving sufficient detail to their progress in communication, social interaction and symbolic behaviour. Does your record system have a framework which does this?
- How could you improve your record-keeping system so that it has an inclusive and integrated approach which is 'multilingual' and uses traditional early childhood educational terms, but also incorporates medical language and will be understood by inspectors?

Further reading

Greenland, P. (2010) 'Physical development'. In T. Bruce (ed.), *Early Childhood: A Guide for Students*. London: Sage. Chapter 16.

Milchem, K. (2011) 'Breaking through concrete: the emergence of Forest School in London'. In S. Knight (ed.), *Forest School for All*. London: Sage.

Stewart, N. (2011) *How Children Learn: The Characteristics of Effective Early Learning*. London: BAECE.

CHAPTER 7

PARENTS AS PARTNERS

> ### In this chapter you will learn about:
>
> - How observing children and their families helps us to see each child as an individual and support them in the best way possible.
> - Linking children's time in the nursery with their time at home.
> - Supporting parents as well as children.

The setting

King's House School is a preparatory school which admits girls and boys at three years old and boys only from four to thirteen years old. It is a non-selective, inclusive school, much valued by parents and the children attending as a school that encourages rather than judges children, seeing them in the round, with excellent results. Children are admitted to the nursery in order of registration, or if they have siblings already in the school. They stay in the nursery for up to two years, which gives children sufficient time to settle and develop their learning with quality.

The school's approach to observation and assessment is discussed in this chapter:

- An induction visit is made prior to starting at the nursery. The observations begin, which inform the settling-in process.
- Then there is a period of settling-in, with staff making careful observations which are shared with parents (i.e. formative assessment).
- There is daily contact with parents at greetings and partings.
- There is also an individual in-tray (a weekly newsletter and weekly bulletin).

- Formative assessment continues through observations made by all staff on sticky labels.
- These are analysed and some are selected weekly to go onto sheets of observations for the term, showing significant markers in a child's progress, that are then shared with parents informally.
- At the end of the first term a summative assessment is made and there is a meeting with parents about the 'Progress Check at three years' which links to the developmental descriptors in 'Development Matters' in the English EYFS framework.
- Clear messages are given to parents about the school's relationship with the EYFS framework.
- Once a term children are encouraged to 'Draw a Man' (Harris, 1963).

What follows is an extract from the school prospectus:

> The Early Years Foundation Stage – King's House School
>
> During the course of your child's time at King's House Nursery, we will be recording his/her learning journey in this personal portfolio. We will make regular observations of day-to-day activities. We will record development milestones, reflect on kindness, courtesy and friendship with others and generally maintain a record against our curriculum guidelines.
>
> We use photographs of your child playing and working alongside other children as valuable evidence of progress in learning.

How the team works

Induction

Children and parents visit the school before the settling-in process begins. During this visit staff will carefully observe a child, and then meet afterwards to discuss how they will work with this family in settling that child into the nursery. (We will see later in the chapter how important these early observations were for Ruby, who was not an easy settler.) When the child begins the parent stays with their child, guided by the staff and helped to withdraw gradually and appropriately according to the individual needs of the child. The Head of the Nursery Sally Crawley describes to parents how children are happy and secure at home, and once they are settled they are secure and feel safe and happy in school. But they find difficult the gap in the middle, namely the transition state of leaving the primary carer (usually their mother) and feeling safe with nursery staff. This needs careful management and individual strategies as no two children or families are the same, although most settle easily using similar approaches for each. (We will see later that Ruby needed more careful and well thought through support, and this paid off.)

Greeting children and parents

We met a group of parents with the Head of the Nursery, Sally Crawley. All were very clear that the presence of the Head greeting them and their children each morning on arrival was invaluable. They spoke about her ability to read situations and how 'She never makes you feel like a silly parent'. She would give a comforting look to a parent after a bad night's sleep, as they were greeted with, as one parent said, 'their precious child'.

Parents feel they can trust her, and that she would act on the snippets of information they often gave her with the wisdom that arises from her professional knowledge. They say that they often tell her things without realising their importance. One mother expressed it this way: 'The waterfall goes straight through, a seamless movement of staff communicating'.

Another parent said Sally and her staff always seem to be one step ahead: 'Sometimes you don't know something is a challenge unless it hits you, but they are already there and thinking about the best way forward'. This has produced a very practical result. Parents feel they can talk to any of the staff, and that they will be well informed about their children because of the way observations are shared.

Parents explain that they feel part of a community. They also feel they are cared for as much as their children. Staff will remind them if they forget for a few days to look in their individual in-tray, which provides information such as the weekly newsletter. This ensures that parents help staff to build on the experiences the children have in the nursery. For example, one week in May the newsletter section from the Nursery Department included the following:

> Our topic this term is Traditional Tales, starting with The Three Little Pigs and Goldilocks and the Three Bears. Good old-fashioned nursery tales are hard to beat!

Children's comments are included when they made porridge:

> This porridge smells yummy.

> This porridge is gooey and sticky – I love it!

> Mummy bear's porridge was too hot, so they went out to the woods for a walk.

Observation

Observation of children and their families is central to the work. Greeting the families is an opportunity to do this, and not only do the parents accept that Sally is engaged in professionally observing them, but they also embrace the way she does so. They are on the receiving end of the results of her observations, shared with her staff, who also observe and share with their colleagues.

The staff team are certain that having high adult:child ratios is fundamentally important to the way they are able to work. Giving children individual opportunities to converse with staff, and to receive individual attention in a sociable atmosphere which encourages communication, is one of the most important aspects of childhood, and if neglected there will be less progress than there could have been. Unfulfilled possibilities are the result of having too many children spending time with too few adults.

Play is valued at King's House. The staff team is proud of the fact that they facilitate learning rather than try to 'teach' the children. This means that there is no need for formal observations of children engaged in adult-set tasks. Staff feel that they can assess the learning of the children in much more depth if they can see how children select what they do, and how they engage in what they do. They have sections in each child's progress check entitled *'next steps'* and *'focus'*. The EYFS developmental descriptors in the EYFS 'Development Matters' are used in each child's profile as a means of identifying next steps for learning. This means that they act on observations to support children's learning and also develop it appropriately.

Sally emphasised, during our discussion with the parents, that observation allows her, with her team, to see the individual strengths and needs of each child, rather than treating the children as a homogeneous group, or expecting children from the same family to be similar in their interests and personalities.

There is much emphasis on staff communicating with each other and sharing observations not only by simply keeping each informed 'as they go', but also through professional discussions with each other. Parents can also come and talk to staff via appointments as well as the daily contact when greeting and parting.

Staff will make observations on sticky labels when they see significant moments in a child's learning, and photography is also a key means of recording and amplifying what is jotted down on the sticky label. Selections are made and inserted in the child's profile booklet, and these are regularly taken home by the family. Children enjoy reflecting on their learning with their parents as they share the book together.

After the first eight weeks there is a three-year progress check, when staff meet the parents and reflect together on a child's learning journey so far. The EYFS is used as a navigational tool in this. This is a two-way exchange. For example Sophie, a mother of twins, gave staff the booklet she had gathered from the Twin Society about non-identical twins to help them work with her sons.

When girls leave King's House and boys move up the school to the reception class, families (who keep the book) are encouraged to show these profile books to the receiving teacher. Children are encouraged to 'draw a man' (Harris, 1963) termly, which is also placed in the profile book.

Why this approach works

Children from the same family will be very different, and should be cared for and educated with this in mind. In this chapter we shall meet three families, all with two children who are, as always, very different and unique. The children are encouraged to be themselves in an atmosphere that helps them to feel that they belong, are secure and feel safe with clear boundaries, surrounded by people who love their company and enjoy spending time with them.

Observing Team Nick and Olly

These three year old non-identical twins arrive at school, having looked at the pirate book they were asked to read at home, and so making links with the pirate theme at school. They come into the classroom and are greeted by a member of staff. They are looking around in a calm, reflective way, and without appearing to communicate with each other, both move in synchrony to the table where they can catch magnetic fish with rods. A member of staff, Issy, notices that they are, after a few minutes, looking around as they fish, and she shows them the possibilities of painting with a string of beads. Olly stays and tries this out, while Nick goes to the paint easel, touching the paint-brush in each pot, but not painting, and then runs to the other end of the room, seeing Hector, and climbs on a large foam soft play prism. He finds a toy car in the small world area, and runs it down the prism, crawling as he goes. Hector picks up a dinosaur and follows Nick, pretending to chase him. The two boys laugh, and enjoy making the car and the dinosaur go down the slope one after the other.

Meanwhile Olly goes to join Sasha at the tray containing circular shapes which can be threaded on rods. They appear to be communicating with each other, but not so they can be heard. They go together to the dough table, where Sasha's twin sister Bella offers Olly a dough cake with a candle on it. He sits between Sasha and Bella, and the three children become engaged in making cakes. Perhaps it is significant that Olly enjoys playing with them. After all, they have common experiences and understandings.

Both at home and in school, Nick and Olly interact with each other very positively with turn-taking, sharing and very little squabbling (although their father did have a little laugh, and suggested that they probably quarrel more at home). But this was not a central part of their interactions with each other. They are clearly deeply attached to one another, which is why their parents describe them as Team Nick and Olly. Their mother laughed and said they are either running or asleep! Nick loves to make Olly laugh as they play together.

The staff observations up until the time of the three-year progress check revealed that there was excellent communication between the boys, but neither staff nor the other children could understand them. They were not hearing language being used. Over one weekend in March the parents wrote copious notes on every word each of the boys said at home. The parents were tuned in to what their children were trying to say.

Examples of the words and phrases Nick used spontaneously were:

'Parkeet' (parakeet)

'Rarrier down' (barrier down)

'Ore ink please' (more drink please)

'Doo shat' (door shut)

'Whale shark' (in school he said 'sha' (shark) on two occasions that were recorded by staff)

Acting on the observations made

Staff responded and recorded the words or near words that they heard each of the boys use. They had a book, and would jot down any words and phrases they recognised during the session.

During March, there were examples of single spontaneous words from Nick:

'Ha' (hat)

'Yeyo' (yellow)

'Stu' (stuck)

and phrases:

'Ou oor' (open door)

'Ge own' (get down)

'Door stu' (door stuck)

By April he was saying 'That go dow' when playing with the garage (that goes down).

This enabled staff to see the individual strengths of each child, rather than Team Nick and Olly. Each had a different word structure and pronunciation. These documented observations at home and in school revealed that Olly used several words while Nick used one with the same meaning. Sophie and Tim (Nick and Olly's parents) emphasised how challenging it had been to note down the words that each of the boys used. The speech and language therapist had stressed the importance of seeing them as different and distinct individuals. Sophie and Tim had discussed whether they should try to learn the language the boys used with each other, and were reassured that staff agreed with their decision to support and encourage them in using conventional English language. The speech and language therapist will now begin to work more intensively with the boys, after seeing them in the classroom context (rather than in an unfamiliar clinic situation).

Figure 7.1   Olly and Nick with beads

The parents and staff began to see heartening progress. The boys had moved from non-verbal communication without sound and no language, although they were empathetic with each other and shared with each other, to using one word utterances. Staff were tuning in.

In school Olly said 'Bore rack rus', which they were able to understand was 'Ball back us'. The ball had rolled back towards them. By April he was saying 'Besh you' when someone sneezed, and 'Going up – now going dow' (down), as well as counting trucks, 'our, ive, ixe' (four, five, six). At home he was asking questions, such as 'Where somewich gone?' (sandwich).

Observations in school suggested that Olly and Nick relied on each other, and chose activities in the nursery to experience together.

They were in fact inhibiting each other in the ability to express verbally. Observations also led staff to see what engrossed and engaged each of the boys. They crawl together quite often. They love dinosaurs and cars, and small world wheeled vehicles. But Nick also loves stacking and balancing objects, and posting. Gradually they were supported by staff in becoming involved in their play without being dependent on the presence of their twin. Their parents were delighted one day, when Olly was sick, and Nick came happily to school without his brother, and was not distressed. He was sufficiently secure by this time in the nursery to feel he belonged. His parents felt that this was facilitated by the wearing of school smocks on which the children chose motifs that appealed to them. Putting on the smock meant going to school. Olly was ill, and so not wearing his smock, so did not go to school. This clarity seemed to be helpful for Nick in his decision that he felt emotionally strong enough to go to school without Olly. The strategy that staff have employed – namely working in close partnership with parents, and facilitating play in order to broaden the skills of each child – had paid off. Olly and Nick began to become engaged in social interaction with other children. The practitioner noted on stick-it labels:

1st May

Nick pushed his bike up to Bella, babbling away to her and pointing around the playground with his finger. Bella listened with interest to what Nick was saying. She gave a nod with her head and said, 'That's ok' before going off to play.

PSED CL PD L M UTW EAD

6th May

Nick loves to post cars, bricks, and balls through the playground railings. Today he played a lovely posting game with bean bags through little holes in the climbing frame. George and Hector were on the other side, posting them back.

PSED CL PD L M UTW EAD

8th May

Olly loved playing with Theo with the bricks today, building a tower together, knocking it down and laughing!

PSED CL PH L M UTW

Figure 7.2   Playing with the brick tower

9th May

Olly having a very happy time with Will in the garden, chasing and catching each other, with lovely two way interaction.

PSED CL PD L M UTW EAD

Nick and Olly had not been happy to join the group at story time, snack time, or other times of gathering. This school encourages play for most of the sessions, but the group times are enjoyable gatherings which encourage participation of a different kind.

Staff began to see Nick and Olly joining in, sitting down, and sharing snack time with other children. Their parents found this very helpful, as coming together and sitting down together to share food reflects their home values. They now sit on a log in Richmond Park on family picnics, which has been a joy to their parents.

> 26th April
>
> Olly sat at the table waiting for fruit and biscuits to come and asked for 'more milk'.
>
> PSED CL PD L M UTW EAD

> 9th May
>
> Joining in with a circle time sound game, trying to guess which animal sound he could hear. 'What is it?', he said with excitement, 'Is cat'. He was engaged with the activity throughout.
>
> PSED CL PD L M UTW EAD

Figure 7.3   Nick and Olly with Mrs Hughes at story time

> 20th May
>
> Nick will sit for a short time with support, listening to a group story. He enjoys stories which use puppets or props.
>
> PSED CL PD L M UTW EAD

The notes made on sticky labels feed into the discussions about each child, and are the base of the formative assessment of the children. At three years there is a summative assessment, the 'Progress Check at three years'. This is shared and discussed with parents, and occurs at the end of the settling-in period of eight weeks. The speech and language therapist will now work with the family and the school, to support and extend the rapid progress Olly and Nick have made, as a result of the teamwork between themselves at home, and with (and between) the staff. The links with the EYFS are demonstrated in the progress charts which follow (Figures 7.4 and 7.5).

The strategies that have worked for Nick and Olly

- Using observation at home and at school to share and dialogue with parents.
- Observation is acted on to find and then extend the interests and needs of Olly and Nick.
- Valuing Olly and Nick as individuals who are different.
- Developing ways for staff to act as a team so that observation can be used effectively to aid development and learning.

Child's Name: Nick	DOB 26.03.10 Age 36 months	Date: March 2013
Personal, Social & Emotional Development		
Self-confidence & self awareness	**Managing feelings & behaviour**	**Making relationships**
• Nick comes happily into the Nursery each morning and is busy from the moment he steps through the door • He explores many different activities but has a definite preference for the cars and trucks and tuff tray resources	• We have seen some improvement at snack time and Nick is now able to stay in his chair and wait for his drink and fruit without wandering off • Nick finds it difficult waiting for his turn and needs support with sharing the toys • Nick still needs a great deal of adult support to follow rules and boundaries	• Nick's close bond with Olly has understandably meant that he has not yet needed to seek out other children • Nick is just beginning to play comfortably alongside other children • Nick has excellent sharing and turn-taking skills with Olly and this should extend to others in time
Developmental Stage: 22–36 months	Developmental Stage: 16–26 months	Developmental Stage: 16–26 months
Communication & Language		
Listening & attention	**Understanding**	**Speaking**
• Nick can maintain attention for a very short time during circle time with adult support • He needs lots of visual cues to help keep him on task • He has a strong exploratory impulse • Nick can concentrate intently on an object of his own choosing for a short period of time	• Nick is not yet responding when he hears his name being called. • Nick needs close adult support to follow instructions	• Nick communicates very effectively with Olly using non-verbal behaviour and his own sounds • Occasionally Nick will use single words when prompted by an adult: 'splash'; 'WOW'; 'red'; 'choo-choo' • Nick is not yet using language to communicate with other children • Nick will choose milk by pointing to the milk jug, but is not yet responding with words
Developmental Stage: 16–26 months	Developmental Stage: 16–26 months	Developmental Stage: 16–26 months

Physical Development

Moving & handling	Health & self-care
• Nick scoots carefully around the garden, developing good control on the three-wheeled scooters • Nick enjoys the wooden trikes, gaining confidence and speed daily! • Nick will spend lots of time transferring pasta or lentils with tweezers or spoons, developing his fine motor skills and concentration	• Nick goes to the bathroom but needs a little help with his clothing • Nick loves the water and always washes his hands after the bathroom • He needs lots of support in the bathroom as he gets easily distracted with door handles and taps
Developmental Stage: 22–36 months	Developmental Stage 22–36 months

Is the child meeting developmental milestones?

Communication and Language skills are only just developing and this will continue to be a key area of focus. We are clearly aware that language skills are often delayed in twins and we will monitor Nick's progress closely.

What next?

Is it possible to have Nick's hearing checked again?

We will encourage language development with books, songs, and conversation.

We will promote sharing and turn-taking with small group games.

We will provide lots of activities that will help to develop Nick's concentration – peg boards; spooning; pouring activities.

Parents' comments, including child's interests:

Figure 7.4 Progress check at three years for Nick

Child's Name: Olly	DOB 26.03.10 Age 36 months	Date: March 2013
Personal, Social & Emotional Development		
Self-confidence & self awareness	**Managing feelings & behaviour**	**Making relationships**
• Olly comes happily into the Nursery each morning and settles quickly to an activity of his choosing • Olly confidently explores different activities throughout the Nursery, particularly enjoying the cars, trucks and water play	• Olly is now able to sit quietly at snack time and will wait patiently for his fruit and drink • Olly has a great sense of humour and will often laugh with an adult in the setting over a shared joke • Olly still needs some adult support to follow rules and boundaries as he is easily distracted by his brother	• Olly obviously has an extremely close bond with his twin brother Nick • Olly is beginning to respond to the attentions of other children, his warm smile often signalling that he is happy to play • Olly is always happy to share toys with Nick and is beginning to do so with other children
Developmental Stage: 22–36 months	Developmental Stage: 22–36 months	Developmental Stage: 16–26 months
Communication & Language		
Listening & attention	**Understanding**	**Speaking**
• We have seen super progress from Olly over the last few weeks. He now settles quickly for circle time and can listen and pay attention to the story when he chooses to • Olly can be easily distracted, but with a bit of adult support will stay on task	• Olly will respond to his name by looking up and acknowledging the adult speaking with a smile • Olly is beginning to respond to simple instructions – 'put away the car'; 'find your coat' • Olly performed well in the Mothers' Day show, by carefully watching the adults and following their prompts. Very well done Olly!	• Olly communicates very effectively with Nick using non-verbal behaviour and his own sounds • Olly will respond to a persistent adult requests with a single word answer 'open'; 'milk'; but is not yet choosing to communicate with words • Olly is not yet using language to communicate with other children
Developmental Stage: 16–26 months	Developmental Stage: 22–36 months	Developmental Stage: 16–26 months

Physical Development

Moving & handling	Health & self-care
• Olly loves outdoor play and rushes outside to find the wooden trikes • Olly loves chasing his brother on the trikes and is often found racing other children down the slope • Olly loves the tuff tray activities – and is often found spooning cous cous or rice into small pots • He enjoys pouring activities at the water tray	• Olly goes to the bathroom, but still needs adult support with his clothing and washing hands • He can identify his coat and will cooperate as an adult helps him to put it on
Developmental Stage: 22–36 months	Developmental Stage: 22–36 months

Is the child meeting developmental milestones?

Communication and Language skills are only just developing and this will continue to be a key area of focus. We are clearly aware that language skills are often delayed in twins and we will monitor Olly's progress closely.

What next?

We will encourage language development with books, songs and conversation.
We will promote language and turn-taking with small group games.

Parents' comments, including child's interests:

Figure 7.5   Progress check at three years for Olly

- Developing trust so that parents and staff can share the more difficult aspects of each child's development as well as celebrating their progress.
- Using the official documents and requirements (EYFS/Ofsted in this English school) as a navigational tool, not as a straitjacket.
- Encouraging friendships with other children and families (e.g. the class picnic to Richmond Park at the weekend which enabled working parents to join home-based parents).

Observing Ruby and acting on the observations

Staff and Ruby's mother thought that Ruby (at just three years old) would settle easily. Her older sister Isla attended the nursery, and Ruby had been brought to take and fetch her for the previous 18 months. Every day she had to be prised away as she seemed to be desperate to attend. However, it became clear when Ruby and her mother attended the induction visit in March, which was an informal gathering for new children and their parents to meet and look around the nursery, that Ruby was anxious, and she clung to her mother throughout. Staff realised that she was going to need sensitive support, and so was her mother. Since there was no blanket settling-in policy or strategies used by staff for settling both children and parents (for both need to feel trust as well as secure), this did not pose a problem. It is often the case that children who have a very strong attachment to their mother find separation very difficult, especially if they have spent time at home together and deeply enjoy each other's company. This is in fact a very positive thing, but Ruby's mother also wanted Ruby to enjoy meeting a wider circle of friends and to be comfortable about meeting new people, thus broadening her social network. Without the careful observations made by the staff at the informal gathering, there would have been an assumption that Ruby would settle into nursery easily. Individual plans were therefore made for her and her mother, as her tears were what the experienced staff described as heartfelt. After less than a month she was showing very positive signs of being settled, providing she could be near adults when she felt the need. She was putting on her smock when she got dressed in the morning, despite attending the nursery in the afternoon.

The formative assessment notes, which plot the progress of each child, are written on the sticky labels available to all the staff, who jot things down at the end of the session or on the spot. However, the emphasis is on working with and actively being with the child, so observation is not allowed to constrain this process. The observations made of Ruby each week (Figure 7.6) show that she is finding things of interest as she settles. An anxious child cannot learn in any depth. Early observations show her alone, but often in companionship with other children, and joining in with group times. She has learnt not to be anxious when her mother has left. The moment of the 'gap', as Sally calls it, when her mother

Ruby Mallinson settling-in

First induction session 20th March 2013
Ruby came in happily with Mum – quite clingy, but happy to explore the creative tables, water and sand trays with Mum by her side.

When members of staff came over to say hello, Ruby was understandably a little shy.

When parents were invited for the Head's introductory talk, children were encouraged to stay and play with staff in the classroom. Ruby was very clingy with Mum and clearly unhappy about being left. She came with Mum into the meeting room; staff commented on the strong attachment to Mum.

Second induction session 24th April
Parents invited to bring children into the classroom and help them to settle with a member of staff, and then leave them for 40 minutes for staff to have the opportunity to get to know the children and vice versa.

Ruby's strong attachment to Mum was again noted by staff and when Mum came to leave, Ruby became very cross and very upset.

SC is most familiar member of staff for Ruby as Ruby accompanies her sister Isla to Butterfly group each morning and is greeted by SC on the door. SC was able to calm and settle Ruby and the rest of the session passed happily with SC keeping Ruby busy with activities.

Ruby was excited to see Mum after 40 minutes play.

At KHN we have no fixed settling-in policy, but tailor our approach to each individual child's needs. In this instance we could see that the hardest part of the session for Ruby was leaving Mum and if we could ensure a smooth handover to a familiar adult, we felt that Ruby would quickly settle into her new routine.

It was agreed that SC should be the key person for handover, given her familiarity with the family and that if Ruby arrived 15 minutes after the other children, then SC should be able to give Ruby her undivided attention.

25th April session 1
Ruby came in for first session, as agreed 15 minutes after the other children.

Ruby was very clingy with Mum; she didn't want to be left.

Mum and staff had agreed that Ruby's handover should be as quick as possible, to avoid any unnecessary anxiety. Ruby showed some resistance but staff worked gently and carefully with Mum and Ruby to minimise any distress. SC cuddled and chatted with Ruby, distracting her with different activities.

The tears lasted three minutes and Ruby was engaged and interested. It was noted that Ruby did not allow SC out of her sight all afternoon.

29th April session 2
Ruby was very clingy with Mum. Insisted on seeing SC and wouldn't let go of Mum until SC was with her. As soon as SC scooped Ruby up, the anger subsided and Mum left without any anxiety from Ruby.

Staff commented on how the attachment had transferred to SC. During the course of the session, SC interacted with other children and left Ruby with MH and IN; Ruby happily played with Nursery equipment; no signs of anxiety.

(Continued)

(Continued)

30th April session 3

A repeat of session 2. Ruby was firmly attached to Mum and reluctant to let go until she had SC's attention. Once that attention was secured, Ruby was very happy to say goodbye to Mum.

SC was only needed for a short while before Ruby relaxed and played happily with MH and IN alongside peers, SC intentionally stepping back a little to allow Ruby to form bonds with other staff, conscious that over-reliance on one staff member is not healthy.

1st May session 4

A repeat. Ruby very clingy with Mum until SC joined in when she cheerily looked up at Mum and said 'bye bye'. Once again SC and MH worked together to include Ruby in group activities, SC stepping back once Ruby relaxed. Staff commented on how Ruby was now forming bonds with all staff members.

2nd May session 5

Ruby settled quickly and happily with IN, her new routine becoming sufficiently familiar that there was no sign of any anxiety or distress.

7th May session 6

Ruby settled herself happily at the creative table; she was so busy with her painting activity that she turned quickly to Mum for a quick 'goodbye'.

She sat happily with IN and then independently moved to the next table to join MH with peers Freddie and Charlie.

She chatted freely 'It's my birthday cake, I got lots and lots of candles'.

Staff observed that Ruby was much more relaxed today; she does like to be close to an adult and enjoys 1-1 when possible.

Figure 7.6   Ruby's settling-in notes

says goodbye, has been dealt with sensitively. She now, after three weeks, feels secure with staff in the nursery, and with the children she spends time with. The practitioner noted the following on sticky labels:

7th May

After a quick handover from Mum, Ruby settled herself into a sticky creative activity. Ruby sat there for a little while happily observing what the children around her were doing.

7th May

Every time Ruby made a snip in the playdough with her scissors she said, 'look'. Ruby was really proud of the marks she had made.

7th May

Ruby – joining in with action songs and pretending to be an elephant and a rabbit during music and movement.

8th May

Ruby had a lovely time playing in the home corner, pretending to feed her mouse with food. She happily plays alongside other children and enjoys it when adults join in her play too.

Figure 7.7   Feeling secure and settling well

There is a leap forward in progress when she dares to try something new to her. She has been choosing activities which are familiar, such as playdough, cutting, and soft toys.

9th May

Not sure about playing with the shaving foam at first. Ruby watched Freddie play for a while before dipping her finger in. She kept wiping the foam off her finger but wanted to have another try. Eventually Ruby ventured further and picked up some sea creatures in the foam to play with.

The strategies that have worked for Ruby

- Ruby was not required to follow the usual settling-in approach because it was clear through staff observations that it would cause her real distress.
- Her mother and the staff worked as a team, with Mum arriving 15 minutes after the other children arrived, so that she entered a calm atmosphere, with children happily engaged in their play.
- Because staff did not let Mum feel anxious, Ruby was surrounded by adults who were confident she would settle happily, which helped her to do so in just over a fortnight. She felt supported both at home and at school.
- A distressed child cannot learn. Ruby was soon able to learn because she felt secure.
- Once she felt secure she found things to interest her which were familiar.
- She needed an adult to be with her, as this helped her to engage with what she was doing and to concentrate.

- She soon felt able to be in companionship with other children without the strain of having to interact. Being at the dough table and playing along-side other children were as much as she could deal with.
- She began to try new things and explore.

Observing Tristan and acting on the observations

Tristan is tall for his age, just like his dad, who stands 6 foot and 8 inches. People sometimes treat him as if he is older than he is. This too was his dad's experience. Tristan has made rapid progress in finding what the staff call his 'control button', and this is celebrated with his parents. When he becomes frustrated, staff are helping him to 'use his words', so that he is beginning to articulate what is worrying him, difficult for him, and what would be helpful for him. Tristan's mother explained to us that this has been an invaluable strategy which has helped her son. She explained how supported she felt by how staff share their observations in ways which help her and Tristan to move forward together. Practitioners noted the following on sticky notes:

> 7th May
>
> 'I have a plaster on because I had a little cut, but Mummy said I can take it off when I go swimming because Mummy says the plaster will come off when I go in the water'.

He is developing an understanding of cause-and-effect. If this, then that happens.

> 7th May
>
> He describes what a day looks like at the nursery, while he is looking at the visual timetable: 'We go to nursery. We stick our names on the board, and then we play and then it's circle time. Sometimes it's 'Little Pup' and music and French, and sometimes after that we wash our hands and it's snack time and then we play outside'.

He is showing the ability to sequence events in time, and very sensibly using the visual timetable as a prompt. This links with his interest in each page of a story book, which guides him through the book and the story.

> 7th May
>
> I like stories because I like looking at all the different pages.

Another aspect of his fascination with sequences is the way he is interested in exploring seriation and classification. His drawings of his family demonstrate how he likes to look at his younger sister, India. He points out her eyes and

Figure 7.8 Tristan's 'My Daddy'

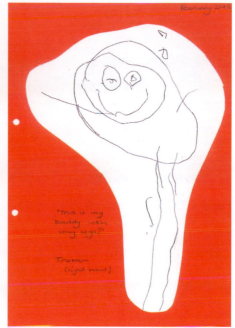

Figure 7.9 Tristan's 'My Daddy with long legs'

her shoes. The top and bottom of her. Beginnings and endings are part of working out seriation through size. He also draws his mummy and daddy (Figures 7.8, 7.9 and 7.10).

Other observations show that he enjoys seriating the number rods 1–5, and is teasing out the mathematical terminology for measurement and weight.

23rd January

'Let's see how much you measure Harry. Oh! I mean how heavy we are! Oops!'

He is interested in classifying objects, and seeing the similarities between them. A cello is like a violin, but bigger.

His fascination with classifying was observed when he enjoyed experimenting with ice in the builder's tray, and seeing 'crystals' and the process of melting (Figure 7.11).

Figure 7.10 India with shoes and eyes

Figure 7.11   Tristan with the ice tray

Tristan is also developing leadership qualities.

22nd January

Tristan leads the way as the afternoon group put on a show for us.

26th April

On hearing a car alarm Tristan shouted, 'Quick, line up, fire alarm!' The children then rushed over and lined up against the wall.

Tristan, through the team work between his parents and the staff at the school, has made great progress in self management, as shown in the links to 'Development Matters' in the English EYFS, in relation to Personal, Social and Emotional Development.

The strategies that have worked for Tristan

- Supporting his mother when she arrives each morning. She describes this as parents needing to feel 'cuddled' as much as the children. The calm approach from staff, and the comforting words, helped Tristan's mother feel confident and to know how to respond to her son.
- Encouraging further support, such as a sleep specialist, to tackle family exhaustion.
- Clear strategies to help Tristan self regulate when he is beginning to feel frustrated, such as saying to him 'Use your words', which has then had a positive impact on his ability to get on with other children and to express his needs. This strategy was easier to put into effect once the sleep problems had been dealt with.
- Celebrating his strengths, such as his way with words, which help him to think at increasingly deep levels.
- Encouraging his leadership skills, whilst supporting him in being caring of others.

What we have learned

- The importance of careful induction and settling-in.
- The importance of greeting each child and family member or carer bringing the child each day.

- The importance of having an in-tray which informs parents and carers (via a weekly newsletter and weekly bulletin).
- Observation is central. Observations that are informal and formative show a child's progress and those aspects which need to be supported and strengthened.
- The summative assessment – the Progress Check at three years – helps staff and parents to take stock regularly.
- Child-initiated learning observations reveal the highest levels of learning.
- Supporting parents as well as children is vital for the social and emotional development of both.
- The gap between is significant – when the child is at home with their family, and then in school with the staff they spend time with, that child feels secure. But the gap in between, the transition from one to the other, also demands careful attention.
- Photos help in profile books with short key messages, highlighting significant markers.
- The importance of using the official framework as a navigational tool (the EYFS in England).
- The feeling of trust between a parent and staff impacts on how a child trusts the nursery staff – in this school, the children give high status to the smocks they wear, seeing them as rites of initiation. They also feel proud when they stay for lunch.
- Staff encourage the development of friendships and encouraging 'play dates' where children visit each other in their homes.
- The concerns parents have often arise from their own childhood experiences. These need to be taken into consideration, with sensitive understanding in developing a positive and respectful relationship between parent and staff.

Reflection on this chapter

- Select three ways in which staff in this school work with parents in partnership, using observation and recording which promote and support the social and emotional development of the children. Discuss with colleagues how you see these connecting with your documentation of the learning of the children in your setting. What will you do as a result?

Further reading

Bruce, T., Meggitt, C. and Grenier, J. (2010) *Childcare and Education* (5th edn). London: Hodder Education. Chapter 7.

Dowling, M. (2010) *Young Children's Personal, Social and Emotional Development* (3rd edn). London: Sage.

CHAPTER 8

OBSERVING AND PLANNING IN THE FOUNDATION STAGE

In this chapter you will learn about:

- The importance of tracking the progress children make as individuals.
- The importance of tracking the progress of groups of children to ensure development.

Details of the setting

Hampton Wick is a rare thing in this day and age. It is an infant and nursery school. This means that it can focus on early childhood education. The school is in a suburban area where there are trees and spaces between houses or blocks of flats and wide streets. It is in huge contrast to the schools and settings in the inner city areas. Hampton Wick Infant and Nursery School has been identified by Ofsted as 'Outstanding'.

Set in this spacious and attractive location, the Headteacher, Heidi Johnson-Paul, is custodian of the small woodland area next to the school which is used as a Forest School area. The children use this area on a regular basis. The garden of the school is seen as an integral part of the classroom, and is used to its fullest. Around every corner there are different areas for climbing, sandpits, reading areas with tables, chairs and logs to sit on to curl up with a book, or do some gardening, etc. It is a very beautiful setting, with a feeling of space. It does not feel crowded or overwhelming despite being a three-form entry school.

Working in close partnership with parents

The importance of working closely with parents is taken very seriously at Hampton Wick. Regular meetings are arranged with each child's class teacher.

Each parent is given a booklet when their child starts school. This, as well as the school website, stresses the necessity of home and school working closely together to support the learning of each child.

The emphasis is always on children making progress, but from time to time it might prove helpful, if a child is not making the progress that is hoped, to have more than a regular discussion with the parents. Then the parent and the school together can think about some specific ways of helping a child to make progress. Suggestions are given in a follow-up letter to the parents so that they can enjoy following things up at home with their child.

Each year a detailed report is sent home to all parents at the end of the summer term. If parents would like to they are encouraged to discuss their child's progress by making an appointment whenever they wish.

Records of individual children

The most vital area of observation, assessing and recording undertaken by the staff lies in the continuous teacher assessment of a child's progress. Each child has a Record which is added to as part of an on-going process. This aims to give an accurate picture of what he or she can do. It is a very positive record. However, as we have seen in the previous section, great care is also taken to identify learning needs which are not being met, so that children do not become constrained in their learning. It is not surprising that the children at Hampton Wick reach higher than national average levels of achievement in literacy and numeracy.

In order to develop the child's Record, each child has a workbook which is an on-going record of the learning and progress which looks at each area of the curriculum. A child's progress is tracked against the age bands in 'Development Matters'. At the end of Reception year attainment is described using the EYFS profile descriptions of 'exceeding', 'expected', and 'emerging' in line with the statutory assessment requirements.

In the Foundation Stage children's progress is tracked against the EYFS using the Early Years Foundation Stage Profile at the end of the Reception class which is part of the legal framework in England.

Each child also has a book called the 'Learning Journey', containing a piece of writing, numeracy and art from each term in Reception until the end of Year 2. It forms a continuous record. The children are given this to keep when they leave Year 2. Because it is an infant and nursery school, they also leave Hampton Wick and go on to their Key Stage 2 junior school. These learning journey records are valued by families, and sometimes become coffee table books, shared with grandparents and others.

The family tapestry

Each year, every family fills in a 'Tapestry' chart called 'Your Child and Their Family' (Figure 8.1). But it is not only the families who do this. The staff also

Figure 8.1 The tapestry chart – 'Your Child and Their Family'

fill in these forms. These are not private. They are shared so that the families as well as the staff have an idea of what interests them. They are used to encourage a feeling of belonging to a learning community.

Gathering observations

In the glossary of this book, we place great emphasis on records which are made on the spot. At Hampton Wick the teachers use 'talk bubbles' to do this, as well as drawings and photography in a digital form, which are then put onto a digitally held record (the child's portfolio). The 'talk bubble' is dated with the child's name and the time of day noted (Figure 8.2).

Drawings

In the Reception class George reports his holiday news. He draws a chicken that is going to hatch an egg. George writes his name spontaneously and without help. He also writes, on his own, 'baby egg' (Figure 8.3).

He tells the teacher:

'This baby egg never cracks'.

'He will put the egg out of his bum'.

'When it cracks it's going to be his birthday, when it's born'.

Evidently George wanted to talk about the chicken before the holiday, and the teacher has noted his deep interest in the subject.

The teacher writes down what he says later. This is an anecdotal recording. It is used to inform the teacher who notes what George has said, and who can then link it with the EYFS.

Photographs and digital record-keeping

Photographs are taken and inserted into a digital portfolio. This holds statements from the Early Years Foundation Stage Profile, which is a requirement as the children are in the Reception class. An observation can be linked to these statements. For example, Siqian is drumming. The portfolio note/observation next to the photograph of her doing this says:

Siqian started beating a beat on the closed playdough box, repetitively. Ratidzo then joined in copying her beat with the rolling pins. Later Angel joined in by rubbing the two rolling pins together to make a different sound. Later, they all added vocals together, 'Yes, yes, yes,

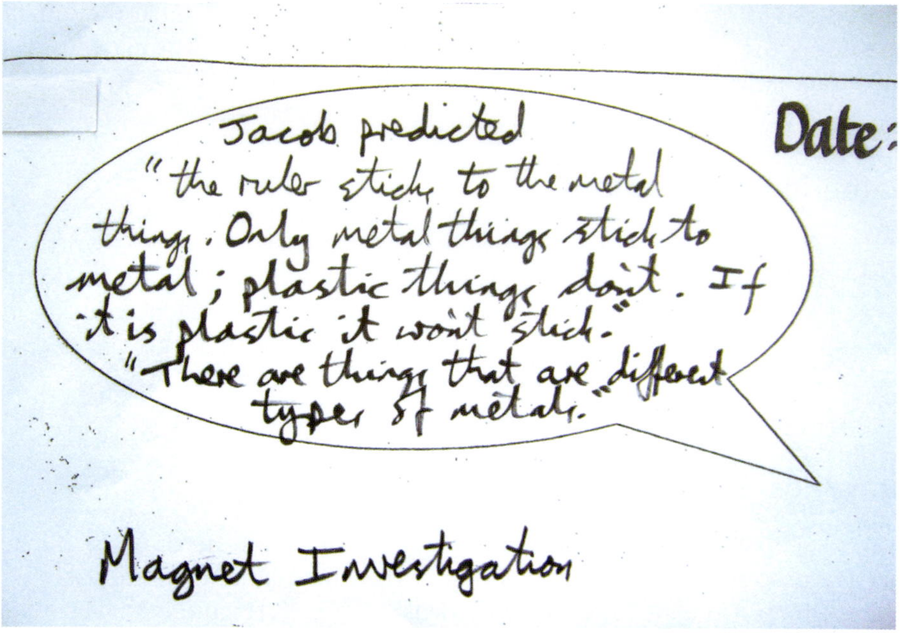

Figure 8.2   The teacher gathers 'on-the-spot' observations during a science investigation using the 'talk bubble'

Figure 8.3   Chicken with egg

yes, yes', in time to the beat. Siqian counted them in, 'One, two, three, go.' Later still Siqian changed the beat to make it faster and organised the others to make sure they were still in time. Later they added more vocals.

This dated observation was then digitally linked to the legally enshrined curriculum framework, with the heading **Aspects contributed to by this experience**:

- **Early Learning Goal:** children play cooperatively, taking turns with others. They take account of one another's ideas about how to organise their activity. They show sensitivity towards others' needs and feelings, and form positive relationships with adults and other children. **Area:** PSED – Making relationships (40–60 months).
- **Early Learning Goal:** children sing songs, make music and dance, and experiment with ways of changing them. They safely use and explore a variety of materials, tools and techniques, experimenting with colour, design, texture, form and function. **Area:** Expressive arts and design – Media and materials (40–60 months).
- Explores the different sounds of instruments. **Area:** Expressive arts and design – Media and materials (40–60 months).
- **Early Learning Goal:** children use what they have learnt about media and materials in original ways, thinking about uses and purposes. They represent their own ideas, thoughts and feelings through design and technology, art, music, dance, role play and stories. **Area:** Expressive arts and design – Being imaginative (40–60 months).
- Maintains attention, concentrates, and sits quietly during appropriate activity. **Area:** Communication and language – Listening and attention (40–60 months).
- Plays alongside other children who are engaged in the same theme. **Area:** Expressive arts and design – Being imaginative (40–60 months).

When children demonstrate that they are consistently and securely performing at 40–60 months, the observations are linked to the Early Learning Goals.

Advantages of electronic forms of record-keeping

Although the aspects contributing to the educational experience of each child are different, the advantages of digital ways of recording progress are that:

- the same photograph can be used in the portfolios of different children all sharing the same educational experience;

- the notes for each child can be the same in each child's portfolio: as we can see from the notes about Siqian, there is also a reference made to Ratidzo and Angel;
- the aspects contributed to by the experience can be linked with the individual child in mind: these will therefore be different in the portfolio for each child;
- there is a section at the end of the portfolio for parent/carer comments to be inserted;
- digital forms of record-keeping are easy to access, and nowadays drawings and examples of writing and mathematical work can be scanned into them.

Disadvantages of digital forms of record-keeping

However, if digital forms of record-keeping are used, it is essential that the practitioners use the technology. The technology must never use the practitioner. A hazard can be that the digital record is designed in such a way that it pushes the practitioner into a strait-jacketed format which constrains what they would like to record and the way in which it has to be recorded.

Recording and acting on information gathered to ensure the progress of groups of children

The Spencer Tracker

This arose out of an urgent need, as schools were becoming overwhelmed by the requirements of Ofsted inspections and the legally enshrined national framework in England of the Early Years Foundation Stage (EYFS). It provides a way of linking the observations gathered as part of the continuous, formative records about each individual child and the requirements, to see how their progress fits within the whole class and the whole school, and in turn with the national picture.

The Spencer Tracker allows teachers to analyse their classrooms to see how children make progress as a group. At a glance teachers can see which languages dominate, or how many children have free school meals, for example. Recent research has shown that faith schools have a lower intake of children on free school meals, for example, across England and Wales. The chart shows numbers of boys and girls, and allows analysis of specific cohorts, such as whether boys and girls are making similar progress in developing mathematical spatial concepts, imaginative aspects, problem solving, etc. These kinds of information inform the planning of the teaching.

Data Gathering, Analysis and Action.
Specific Cohort: Children With EAL

Name	Class + Year	Stage of Development	Language(s) Spoken	Level of Achievement	Level of Support Allocated Provision December 2012	Action Required
	RH	2	Chinese	LA	S&L / EAL focus – 1x week 15 mins teacher, 1:4 Literacy focus – 1x week 15 mins teacher, 1:7	*Continue to provide opportunities for speaking and listening *Focus group support to develop segmenting/blending *Focus group support to develop expressive and descriptive language skills *Monitor development of language
	RH	4	Italian	HA	None needed	*Continue to provide opportunities for speaking and listening *Monitor development of language
	RH	2	Shona	LA	S&L / EAL focus – 1x week 15 mins teacher, 1:4 Literacy focus – 1x week 15 mins teacher, 1:7 Numeracy focus – 1x week 15 mins teacher, 1:5	*Continue to provide opportunities for speaking and listening *Focus group support to develop segmenting/blending *Focus group support to develop expressive and descriptive language skills *Focus group support to develop number recognition, ordering, counting and conservation of number *Monitor development of language
	RH	4	German	MA	None needed	*Continue to provide opportunities for speaking and listening *Monitor development of language
	RH	2	Dari Persian	MA	S&L / EAL focus – 1x week 15 mins teacher, 1:4 Literacy focus – 1x week 15 mins teacher, 1:7	*Continue to provide opportunities for speaking and listening *Focus group support to develop segmenting/blending *Focus group support to develop expressive and descriptive language skills *Monitor development of language
	RH	4	Albanian/ Shqip	HA	None needed	*Continue to provide opportunities for speaking and listening *Monitor development of language

(Continued)

(Continued)

Hampton Wick Infant and Nursery School
Specific Cohort: Gifted and Talented

Name	Class + Year	Presenting Gift or Talent	Level of Achievement	Level of Support Allocated Provision December 2012	Action Required
	RH	Mathematics	HA	To extend through differentiated activities, questioning and problem solving.	Monitor progress through class assessment and observations.
	RH	Understanding the World	HA	To extend through differentiated activities, questioning and problem solving.	
	RH	Literacy	HA	To extend through differentiated activities, questioning and problem solving.	

Figure 8.4 English as an additional Language, Spencer Tracker

Specific Cohort: Minority Ethnic Groups

Name	Class + Year	Minority Ethnic Group	Level of Achievement	Comparisons with Class Cohort	Level of Support Allocated Provision March 2013	Action Required
	RH	Mixed – White and Black African	MA	Average	None needed	*Continue to provide opportunities for speaking and listening *Monitor development of language
	RH	Chinese	LA	Below average	S&L / EAL focus – 1x week 15 mins teacher, 1:4 Literacy focus – 1x week 15 mins teacher, 1:7	*Continue to provide opportunities for speaking and listening *Focus group support to develop segmenting/blending *Focus group support to develop expressive and descriptive language skills *Monitor development of language
	RH	Black/Black British – African	LA	Below average	S&L / EAL focus – 1x week 15 mins teacher, 1:4 Literacy focus – 1x week 15 mins teacher, 1:7	*Focus group support to develop segmenting/blending *Focus group support to develop expressive and descriptive language skills
	RH	Black/Black British – African	LA	Below average	S&L / EAL focus – 1x week 15 mins teacher, 1:4 Literacy focus – 1x week 15 mins teacher, 1:7 Numeracy focus – 1x week 15 mins teacher, 1:5	*Continue to provide opportunities for speaking and listening *Focus group support to develop segmenting/blending *Focus group support to develop expressive and descriptive language skills *Focus group support to develop number recognition, ordering, counting and conservation of number *Monitor development of language

(Continued)

(Continued)

Name	Class + Year	Minority Ethnic Group	Level of Achievement	Comparisons with Class Cohort	Level of Support Allocated Provision March 2013	Action Required
	RH	White – any other background	MA	Average	None needed	*Continue to provide opportunities for speaking and listening *Monitor development of language
	RH	Asian/Asian British – any Asian background	MA	Average	S&L / EAL focus – 1x week 15 mins teacher, 1:4 Literacy focus – 1x week 15 mins teacher, 1:7	*Continue to provide opportunities for speaking and listening *Focus group support to develop segmenting/blending *Focus group support to develop expressive and descriptive language skills *Monitor development of language
	RH	White – any other background	HA	Above average	None needed	*Continue to provide opportunities for speaking and listening *Monitor development of language
	RH	Mixed	HA	Above average	None needed	*Continue to provide opportunities for speaking and listening *Monitor development of language

Figure 8.5 Minority ethnic groups Spencer Tracker

Examples of specific cohorts are:

Free school meals, English as an additional language, special educational experience, ethnicity, gifted and talented, attendance, pre-school experience.

The tracker also allows analysis of the progress of children as individuals and children as a specific group in the prime and specific areas of the English EYFS.

A great deal of attention is given to the way that different groups of children progress in their learning. This is where the Spencer Tracker is proving to be invaluable. It is now widely used, and practitioners are finding it to be an excellent support in tracking the progress of children such that trends can be identified in relation to particular groups of children, as well as individual children. This makes it possible to see, in ways which are accurate and easy to do, if groups of children (for example those with Special Educational Needs or English as an Additional Language, or children who are summer born, to name a few) are making progress. Do girls and boys progress in learning to read and write in similar ways? Are the children being encouraged to be creative? Are they feeling secure and enjoying their time at school? Knowing about these different aspects helps the teachers to be informed, and to act on what they find out.

An example of the way in which data about a specific cohort of children is gathered, using the Spencer Tracker, can be seen in relation to Children with English as an Additional Language (Figure 8.4).

Another example of a specific cohort is that of minority ethnic groups (Figure 8.5). Using the Spencer Tracker, as with any group, this can be looked at across the school as a whole and in a more granular way with finer detail within individual classes. This is very helpful, especially if the population and demographic of an area change, and so there are differences at different points in the school. Once teachers focus on gathering data about the groups of children they work with as well as the individual children they teach, the whole process becomes fascinating, and very educationally worthwhile. But the system used to gather the data needs to be user friendly and accessible. It should not become a burden, or it will not be enjoyed and appreciated; it will become a duty and a tedious exercise. The Spencer Tracker avoids these problems.

The charts have been anonymised. It is important to note the carefully recorded action required. In this way care is taken to give the right support at the right time in the right way for individual children.

It is also important for staff using the Spencer Tracker to be adequately trained (see further reading at the end of the chapter) and to be confident in its use.

Assessment and accountability

Jan Dubiel is an internationally regarded expert in assessment. In his (2014) book, he emphasises the importance of practitioners holding in their minds, hearts and practice the purpose of assessment. Assessment should support the development and learning of a child and also support the teaching which enables this:

> Decisions about what is assessed and how this information is gleaned need to be dependent on the practitioner who is taking them, and should not be subject to compromise and dilution from external pressures. (Dubiel, 2014: 7)

The everyday observations and interactions which take place are the main source of the kind of observations which lead to accurate and reliable assessment. Continuous assessment is key, because it is based, as Jan Dubiel makes clear, on practitioners' knowledge of a child across a range of situations and educationally worthwhile experiences.

This is not to say that there should be no accountability. It is just that the most responsible kind of accountability arises when those who are accountable are committed to the work they do, emotionally engaged in doing the best they can, and well educated and trained in doing so:

> ... practitioners will need to be aware that external accountability, in a range of forms, will be required at different points and from different perspectives and agendas. This type of accountability, although appropriate and valid, needs to be driven and articulated by the existing assessment that practitioners use, and should not create specific ways or models to do this that are not usable within their own accountability and cannot be used to support on-going practice. (Dubiel, 2014: 9)

Observations of children need to demonstrate that they are doing something consistently and independently across a range of situations. This means that children need to be educated in rich learning environments both indoors and outdoors.

This also requires training practitioners in child development. This is becoming increasingly vital as research (Malloch and Trevarthen, 2009, Ockelford, 2013) reveals more and more about brain development. This suggests an holistic approach, because what is emerging is the importance of social relationships and sensory learning as keys to learning.

Children need to learn with, from and through practitioners who are able to make observations which will inform them about a child's progress and facilitate the planning of next steps and general approaches for a group in taking the learning forward, but also crucially here, deepening the learning and making sure it becomes secure.

In this sense, 'next steps' is an unfortunate phrase. Planning should take children deeper and deeper where they are, and does not always involve moving onwards and upwards. The Scottish *Curriculum for Excellence* understands this. Depth and breadth are valued as well as moving on. The Te Whāriki curriculum in New Zealand is exemplary in recognising the significance of a time of plateau in learning, when children stay where they are and consolidate their learning.

Friedrich Froebel, the pioneer educator of the nineteenth century, put this well:

Let us live with our children. (1886: 92)

Practitioners who have difficulty in relating to the children they work with will also have difficulty in observing and assessing what they see. If people do not enjoy their work, and the people they work with (in this case children), it may be wise to consider another career. For those who do enjoy the company of young children and find it fascinating hearing the things they say, the imagination and creativity they show, their determination to solve problems and their joy in movement and stories, dance and music, there is no more rewarding work, and observation that informs planning is then the icing on the cake. Both initial training and continuing professional development play a key part in this. Developing a professional attitude means developing an internal energy to be accountable and striving to create the best education a child can be offered.

When external accountability cuts into and undermines, it can do untold damage. Quality of education does not result. The respected motto of Her Majesty's Inspectorate (HMI) used to be, 'Do good as you go'. Those who hold power need to keep this in mind, for the sake of the children we educate. Otherwise, schooling can constrain a child's education.

What we have learned

- In a large primary school it is important to have systems for gathering observation which inform planning and address issues of accountability which work with clarity, effectively and without becoming an unbearable burden.
- Accountability will have external aspects, but it is vital that these are not the starting point in a school. Assessment is first and foremost how practitioners support the learning and progress of a child's development and learning.
- The physical learning environment needs to be made from a wide range of materials indoors and out of doors. This needs to be constantly sustained, monitored and added to in the light of observations.

(Continued)

(Continued)

- Practitioners need to be trained in child development in order that they can observe and act on significant markers in each child's developing learning.
- Practitioners also need to be able to link their observations to legally enshrined requirements in ways which chime with the approach to pedagogy outlined above. This needs to be practically possible, useful to the main work of the school in educating children, and also user friendly, parent friendly and accessible.
- The use of digital electronic systems is helpful, providing the format does not constrain the approach to observation through the application of an understanding of child development and what constitutes rich learning environments. Technology should be used. It should not use the practitioner by placing observations and links to official documents into a narrow straitjacket, or a pedestrian approach to children's development and learning.

Reflections on this chapter

- Do you use digital electronic ways of gathering observations and linking these to official documents?
- If not, would it be worth investigating how to do this in ways that keep faith with your time-honoured approach to early childhood education?
- If you do, are you sure that the format you use encourages you to make full use of your continually developing understanding of child development? And of the importance of using observation to inform planning? And the fact that education is constrained if the learning opportunities take place in a narrow curriculum?
- Do you have easy ways to use an electronic tracker system to look at children's progress, such as the Spencer Tracker?

Further reading

Dubiel, J. (2014) *Effective Assessment in the Early Years Foundation Stage*. London: Sage.

Moylett, H. (ed.) (2014) *The Characteristics of Effective Early Learning: Helping Children Become Learners for Life*. Maidenhead: Open University Press.

Moylett, H. and Stewart, N. (2013) *Emerging, Expected, Exceeding: Understanding the Revised Early Years Foundation Stage Profile*. London: Early Education/ BAECE.

The Spencer Tracker. Available from Dr John Spencer Publications.

CHAPTER 9

OBSERVING AND SHARING PRACTICE

In this chapter you will learn about:

- Observation as a way of looking at and adapting practice in different settings.
- How to create a rich learning environment with sustainable materials.
- The importance of building on the strengths of the community rather than beginning with what is lacking.

Details of the setting

The Froebel Trust project in Soweto, South Africa is well established. The staff at Soweto have embraced the opportunity to develop the physical environment, working together with the Froebel Trust team to create a sustainable learning environment which is culturally appropriate.

The routine of the day

The children arrive at breakfast time, and when they have gathered in the classrooms, brought by parents or relatives, the older children attend an assembly outside. They dance and sing with the staff. The youngest children, between one and two years of age, remain in their classrooms.

The children are provided with breakfast, and then the day of lessons begins. There are about 50 children in each room, with about 30 one year olds. There are now two members of staff with each group of children.

After lunch, also provided by the Social Development Agency feeding programme, the children sleep on the floor of the room, and then go outside to play.

Founding principles

The Soweto project is based on two major approaches which guide the practice both of the Froebel Trust team, and the staff at the nursery.

1. Traditions of the Froebelian approach to education

The team from the Froebel Trust use the Froebelian principles to guide their practice. Friedrich Froebel first expressed these principles in the mid-nineteenth century, but they have been developed over time. A modern presentation of some of the most important principles was developed by Bruce (1987) but this has been updated through a process of continual review in order to reflect current priorities.

This means that instead of being rigid and outdated, the Froebelian principles are constantly adapted through reflective debate and adjustments in practice, and have become a way for practitioners to continue to create learning opportunities for themselves and the children they care for. The Froebelian principles have proven to be invaluable in working in a different cultural context, and have helped the team to avoid imposing their own culture on the setting and to communicate and work with staff appropriately and effectively.

Key Froebelian principles

- Childhood is part of life, and not simply preparation for it.
- The whole child is considered to be important. Health, physical and mental, is emphasised, as well as the importance of feelings, relationships, thinking and spiritual aspects.
- Learning is not compartmentalised, for everything links.
- Intrinsic motivation, resulting in child-initiated and self-directed activity, is valued.
- Self-discipline is emphasised.
- There are especially receptive periods of learning and sequences of development.
- What children can do (rather than what they cannot do) is the starting point for children's education.
- There is an inner life of the child, which emerges under favourable conditions, such as pretending and imagining through play.

- The people (both adults and children) with whom the child interacts are of central importance.
- The child's education is seen as an interaction between the child and the environment, including the physical, materials, other people and knowledge itself. (Bruce, 1987: 2014)

2. The Asset Based Community Development approach (ABCD) embedded in Appreciative Inquiry

This approach aims to empower communities through collective reflection, communication, and discovering common ground, energy and caring about each other.

The founding Principal of the crèche and school (the late Pam Mfaxa) was a respected leader who had worked since 1991 with a deep commitment to her community.

She was clear during initial conversations that her dream was to be able to offer the children in the crèche and school a curriculum similar to that of children in countries such as the USA, the Nordic countries and the UK, which she regarded as being highly desirable. This remarkable woman, Pam Mfaxa, had recently attended the Community Leadership Development course pioneered by Professor Ian Bruce CBE through seed corn funding from the Joffe Foundation, working with Professor Hanna Nel at the University of Johannesburg.

But would it have been appropriate for the Froebel Trust team to have worked with Pam on what she desired – a UK early childhood curriculum? Imposing and transmitting what works in one culture and inserting it into another very different culture in a different part of the world does not work. It also implies arrogance on the part of those doing the imposing and transmitting.

This is where the ABCD approach, to which Professor Hanna Nel introduced the Froebel Trust team, proved to be invaluable. The Froebelian principles and the ABCD approach were found to chime with each other in very helpful ways. The ABCD approach was developed by Kretzmann and McKnight (1993) (Asset Based Community Development Institute, Illinois). Instead of beginning with a focus on problems, deficits and a lack of resources and training, with external support being central, ABCD emphasises the assets and strengths within the community as the starting point, which does not create a long-term dependency on external support for sustainability. Instead this approach encourages an appreciation and mobilisation of the positive assets and strengths for both individuals and communities. The aim is to uncover concealed gifts through Appreciative Inquiry (Cooperrider and Whitney, 2001) and to facilitate vision through dream, design, delivery and discovery.

The aims of the project

Pam and her staff were therefore encouraged to identify their strengths. These were the fact that the children will learn several of the 11 official languages of South Africa, including English, by the time they are 6 years of age. Children will usually learn their first language, for example Xosa, Zulu or Sithu, then pick up other languages, and after that begin to learn English. Singing and dancing are a strong part of the traditions of the school. Singing in harmony, in different languages, is not something that the Froebel Trust team could offer.

The Principal wanted the children in her school to be offered a Western type of curriculum (such as the British Nursery School). But the Froebel Trust staff were anxious not to impose an inappropriate curriculum which would not be sustainable, and which would undermine the strengths of the community and culture. There was an interesting discussion. It was evident that the Froebel Trust team were mono-lingual, and they were not a patch on the staff as far as singing and dancing were concerned. To impose a curriculum which did not take account of these strengths would be a great loss to the community.

Through discussions the staff began to feel a sense of pride in their strengths, which had not been something they had felt previously, as far as an early childhood curriculum was concerned.

Design

It takes time and a great deal of discussion and the development of trust in each other to move from a dependency model to an ABCD approach. The emphasis on the part of the Froebel Trust was on offering training in the form of practical work with the staff and children, and constant discussion, reflection and review. Both the Froebel Trust team and the staff at the crèche/school were in a continual state of learning. This is the best kind of training.

Parents and helpers organised by Pam were paid to be in the classrooms so as to release staff members for training when necessary. Staff then played with the materials they would be using with the children and talked about their value. The caretaker would often participate in the training for part of the time.

The materials offered were sustainable, which chimes with the Froebelian approach to early childhood education. Many of them were developed from revisiting the materials used in the early nursery schools at the turn of the nineteenth century in the UK, because they offer children worthwhile educational opportunities at a low cost. Modern-day materials that were low cost were also added.

The only materials that were high cost were those that would be sustainable. Again, looking at the early nursery schools, the use of wooden blocks (Froebel's Gifts), although expensive to buy, can last for half a century if cared for.

The materials offered included:

- Mark making materials:

  o portable individual slate boards and chalk;
  o blackboard paint on the walls.

- Malleable materials:

  o clay;
  o plastic wipeable mats;
  o overalls that could be wiped clean;
  o washing-up bowls to wash hands (there was no running water in the school apart from in the kitchen).

- Soft sphere on a string:

Figure 9.1   Clay

  o these can be made of string and are invaluable for use with babies and toddlers: they are Froebel's first Gift.

- Construction using balance and freestanding materials:

  o wooden blocks to use on the floor; the wooden blocks are also Froebel's Gifts.

- Construction materials with connecting parts that are not free standing:

  o coffee sticks and bluetack lumps (to echo the stick and peas used in the early nursery schools): it was decided not to use food materials as the children are nourished using a kitchen funded by social services.

- Sand:

  o dustpans and brushes;
  o child-height besom brooms (adult size with handles shortened);
  o at first seed boxes of sand were introduced to use on the tables, but the staff found this unacceptable. As children sleep on the floors, it was too gritty even when swept up carefully. After two years staff introduced sand in the garden, placing it in upturned broken plastic

tables, and placing it at the base and underneath two climbing frames that had been donated. This means the sand does not turn to mud when it rains, which it does, heavily. It is under the frame and so protected. The sand in the table frames is located on the verandah, and is used by the one to two year olds.

- Paper folding materials:
  - newspapers were collected and children made aeroplanes with them in the garden: other paper folding possibilities are shown in Figure 9.2 below.

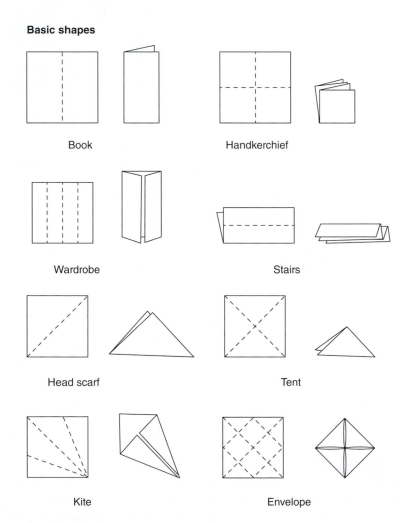

Inspired by Heinrike Schauwecker-Zimmer
(Source: International Froebel Society Conference, Jena, 2011)

Basic shapes

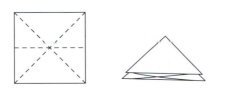
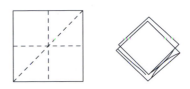

Paper glider triangle   Inside reverse square

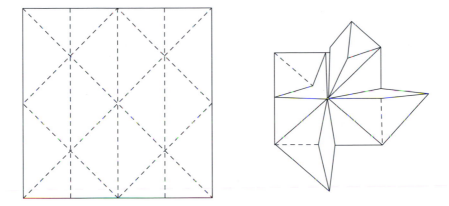

Tablecloth

Figure 9.2   Paper folding

(*Source:* Heinrike Schauwecker-Zimmer)

- Pin boards, peg boards and tessellation boards:
  - like the paper folding these are some of Froebel's Occupations;
  - children make shapes using elastic bands wrapped round the pins on the board;
  - they insert the pegs into the holes on the peg board;
  - the tessellation boards are made of triangles and diamond shapes;
  - these pieces of equipment will last for many years, providing the pegs are carefully looked after: only the elastic bands will need renewal.

Delivery

The story of the introduction of the sand into the garden, and not into the classroom, illustrates the style of the delivery of the training.

The **aim** was to develop the curriculum in ways which:

- were right for the community;
- would not make them reliant on external funding.

The **design** was to celebrate and extend the strengths of the curriculum that already existed. It was also to introduce materials that were sustainable, and to train the staff in order that they could be empowered to use them in ways that both educated the children to maximum effect and helped them to be reflective practitioners.

The Froebel Trust team each took on different roles: Stella Louis led the training; Georgie McCall led the classroom organisation that was necessary for implementing the training; Tina Bruce supported the team.

For the **delivery**, each day the staff would meet in the garden for training led by Stella. Staff used the materials as a group, working with the member of the Froebel Trust who led the training, and supported by the two other members of the Froebel Trust team. There was a different focus each day. For example, for one session they would play with the blocks, while on another day they would use the clay, or mark make with the slates, construct with the sticks, or make patterns with them. Stories were introduced, attempting to use African stories. The staff would act them out and there would be plenty of discussion.

The staff and training team would then go into a classroom and try things out. As we saw, the sand was rejected for two years. The Froebel Trust team never wished to impose. The training was an offering. How it was taken up or not was not for them to decide.

At first the key member of staff working with the one year olds was not included in the training. It became clear that this was because she did not speak English. It was felt important that she should join, and because the sessions were always very practical, she was able to join in and on occasions to lead. Her storytelling and acting abilities were impressive.

During these training sessions there was a great deal of **observation** of how different members of staff operated. The Froebel Trust team participated with the staff, led by Stella. For example, with the stick and blu tack session, one member of staff made football goalposts, and discovered the importance of the triangle. She did not want to dismantle her model (a feeling which many children experience) and so we moved it onto a board and she showed it to the children. This was at the time of the Football World Cup, so the children were very interested in the model.

This led to further staff discussions about the importance of teaching mathematics so that children could see the relevance of shapes such as triangles, which are extremely useful in engineering and architecture amongst other things. Teaching others begins with our own learning. There is a saying, 'If you only do what you've always done, you will always do what you've always done'. This is not conducive to curriculum development.

Observation allows us to consider our own learning, and practically try out what makes us learn, therefore turning us into reflective practitioners.

Delivering storytelling

At the end of the training session, the three and four year olds and then the five and six year olds (a class of nearly fifty children at a time) were invited to be the audience. The Froebel Trust team wanted the staff to tell the stories and act them out in their first language (Zulu, Xosa or Sithu). This was based on research evidence showing that children learn other languages best if they are able to use their first language. Strength in this enables them to think better, and this in turn helps the child to understand how other languages work. Initially, however, the dream of the children learning English in school over-rode this, and so the story was told in English. The children concentrated hard, and enjoyed the story. But suddenly, one of the staff decided to ask her colleagues to act the story again, this time with her narrating it in Zulu. This time the children whooped with joy at various points in the tale, and called out in anticipation of what would come next.

The discussion between the Froebel Trust team and the staff was buzzing that day. Was the children's excitement because they already knew the story when it was told in Zulu because they had already been told it in English first? Was it because they understood the language that they could engage with it more deeply (Bloch, 2013)? Or should children learn all their lessons in English in school because this was a passport to a well-paid job later on? Did it matter that the staff were telling the story in their third language (Russell, 2010) when they spoke in English, and did this affect the quality of their storytelling?

This discussion has some interesting aspects, which need to be reflected upon. Part of the strength of the curriculum in Soweto has been identified in the singing and dancing, and multi-languages which are taught through a whole group experience. The children stand in rows with the teacher at the front. There is a lot of call and response, repetition and movement with rhythm which helps to say the words. This is also how the children learn English. They chant, and give rote learnt responses.

The adult chants, for example, 'What is this?'

The children reply, 'This is a triangle'.

A child is asked to select the triangle on the wall, saying, 'This is a triangle'.

The adult asks, 'Is he right?'

The children call out as a chant, 'He is right. It is a triangle'.

The Froebel Trust team were anxious not to interfere with this aspect of the curriculum because the power of the group is part of the community feeling, and we did not wish to undermine the cultural traditions and perhaps the very strengths we were hoping to build on through the ABCD approach. However, staff were commenting on the way the children used triangles in their stick and blu tack constructions, their pattern boards and shape boards, as well as in their blockplay. The children were using triangles for a purpose but needed to be given the mathematical term 'triangle'. Only when engaged in the practical work did the formal chanting lesson on the triangle have any meaning or make any sense.

As a result the Froebel Trust team decided to enhance the storytelling, song and music. We expanded the stories and songs so that the children had English songs and stories told in English after they were told in the first language.

Delivering wooden blockplay

As always, the staff were introduced to the blockplay first, before introducing the children to the blocks. This was essential, as they began to see the potential of the materials. They made football goalposts and palaces, and discussed how to make a roof or how to build tall. They considered the need for a flat surface, and how important it was to have enough blocks to make what you wanted to make. They talked about being made to share, when the other person has a completely different idea of what they would like to make. They complained about people taking the very block you wanted to use and not having enough time, and discussed being allowed to experiment and choose what to make. They thought it important to locate the blocks away from people walking through.

Following on from this the staff and the Froebel Trust team went into the classrooms of the older children to observe them being introduced to the blocks, and how they used them. It was important to persuade the staff not to show the children what to do. When they stood back they began to see that the children had ideas, and were keen to experiment. By the third year of our sessions together, there was a new room to be used for blockplay, so that all the blocks and home corner pretend play materials were in the one place.

The blockplay is at a higher level of quality than much of the blockplay in the UK. The children from the three and four year old room and the five and six year old room use this space for their learning as well as their classroom and the verandah onto which the classrooms open.

Observing children at play with the wooden blocks

A group of children playing with the wooden blocks chatted together in their first language, and a building emerged that looked impressive. A child told the practitioner that it was the Carlton Hotel. They then had a party, and danced round it.

Several things of significance were mulled over at the staff discussion:

- One child, a boy of five years, led the play and was very verbal in his first language.
- Another four year old boy was very practical and good at solving any problems that arose as the construction developed.
- He discovered the arch, which is a fundamental and significant marker in blockplay development.
- Staff observed the care children took not to knock the blocks down, and to place each block with this in mind.
- They worked as a team.
- The fact that this was the Carlton Hotel meant they were functioning at a symbolic level in their pretend play.
- The Carlton Hotel is also of deep cultural significance as it is where the ANC (African National Congress) had their first legally permitted meeting after apartheid. Hence the celebration with the party.
- A younger girl of three years old had needed an adult to be with her, alongside, while she made an enclosure with the blocks. She had an idea, but did not have the confidence to work without the comforting presence of an adult next to her.

At Soweto written records are not kept of each child's progress (which is not surprising given the large size of classes, the level of training of the staff and the lack of paper). But staff are now discussing the progress of **individual children**, rather than offering the curriculum with an

Figure 9.3

Figure 9.4

Figure 9.5

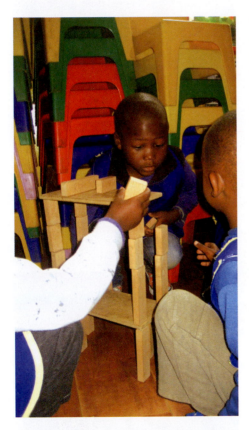

Figure 9.6

entirely whole group approach. Observation is the key here. It has helped the staff to plan how to offer the children educationally worthwhile learning experiences. In other words, the observations informed the planning. They also led to staff beginning to reflect on and question their current methods of learning and teaching.

It is one thing to know how you would like to teach children, but it is quite another to put this into effective practice. The Froebel Trust staff worked with the staff of the crèche and school by going into their classrooms immediately following the training sessions with different sustainable materials. But this would not have been enough. It was also necessary to discuss practical problems as they began to emerge, after the first introduction of a material.

Using observations to develop provision

Georgie McCall supported staff in the one year old room, the two and three year old room, and the three and four year old room.

The 'baby' room as it was known, although most children there were walking, was a place where children were not left to cry, and would be changed and fed, but this loving atmosphere took all the energy and time of the two staff with the thirty or so children. Observations of the room in action, alongside the training sessions, led to the decision that there was little to stimulate the children. They milled about with little to do as a result.

Sustainable materials were introduced, and the children were observed using them. Small empty plastic water bottles were filled with objects so that they became shakers. Some were filled with water and glittery materials to shake. Pieces of cloth were used to make dens to hide in, cardboard boxes were to sit in, bowls were to be used as play props. The walls were painted with blackboard paint so that the children could mark make on them with chalk.

The children were allowed out onto the verandah to sit in the upturned table and play with the sand. The potties were placed on the verandah so that they could watch. The old shed became a changing room and the children loved this room.

The two rooms for the two and three year olds and the three and four year olds have a connecting door. One room is dark and small and is next to the kitchen. The staff have different styles of working, but over time they have begun to open the door between the rooms, and to set out materials so that the children can move across the two rooms when making their choices of what to do.

As a result of the sessions on storytelling, the staff have developed a system where the smaller classroom is no longer a route through to the kitchen. They wanted the children not to be disturbed.

In each room of the crèche/school, the children have an area for pretend domestic play. They play with tea cups, soft toys and dolls donated by visitors at various times. There are upturned cardboard boxes for tables and beds for dolls. Offcuts of materials are used to make slings to carry the 'babies' on their backs. Staff observe how children imitate adults in their families, preparing food and carrying their babies to the market. Some children simply do as the others do, and some lead the play. They become characters, who prepare meals and interact with the others. Pretend play is a significant marker in a child's learning journey. It is impressive to see how the staff observe and know their children in these respects.

The door to the garden is now open, and the children walk past the organic vegetable garden developed by the caretaker, encouraged by Georgie McCall who has vegetable growing areas for each classroom in the garden of her school in the UK. In the garden the staff have made a home corner fantasy area, as they call it, in a shed. This is particularly popular with the two and three year olds, who are emerging into domestic home play. There is now a large sand pit, made by the caretaker with the enthusiasm of the Principal (Figure 9.7). Again, Georgie was able to give sound advice on drainage, a tarpaulin cover and the safety of the edges, drawing on her experience as a head teacher.

Figure 9.7 Children enjoying the sandpit

Staff development through study visits to the UK

It became clear that the Principal and her staff had become reflective practitioners, eager to dialogue with colleagues working in a different cultural context, but increasingly confident in the way they found it best to practise in their own cultural context.

Over the next three years, different members of staff were funded by the Froebel Trust to spend a week in three London nursery schools/children's centres. This led to a different kind of discussion. Georgie and Stella were travelling tutors working with them in the schools.

They saw luxury in the equipment and the materials (paint, paper, expensive felt pens, pencils, etc.) offered to the children which would not be sustainable on the non-existent budget in their crèche/school. But this was not allowed to get in the way of observing what they found to be common to both cultural contexts.

They saw sand, water play, clay, and recycled materials such as boxes and bottle tops being used.

They felt a sense of pride in realising that their children also experienced construction play through the sticks and Blu Tack.

They were impressed that their children had wooden blocks, and appreciated this in the light of the cost of providing them. They take great care of these expensive items.

They had some of the Froebel Occupations which were not in use in the nurseries they visited (tessellated shape boards; pin boards).

The Principal, on her visit, was impressed with the food children were offered. A nutritionist had developed a menu for Georgie in her school, and this was taken for use. There were several vegetarian days in the menu, which were of high nutrition and cheaper to provide. On returning to Soweto, the Principle was determined to have a better kitchen in her school, and secured funding for this.

There was great interest in the way children with disabilities and special educational needs were educated in the UK. A little girl with Down's Syndrome remained in the 'baby' room despite being three years old in the Soweto setting, because that would be the traditional approach. Georgie shared and explained the practice with the visiting staff. On the next visit of the Froebel Trust team, the little girl was in her correct year group, and fully participant in it. She is now in the mainstream primary school. This is a very good example of, 'If you always do what you've always done you'll always do what you've always done'. Sometimes seeing something done in a different way causes the kind of thinking that brings about a change of practice. This is the value of observing practice in different countries and different types of settings. The Froebel Trust team also had to rethink much of their practice because of their observations of practice in Soweto.

What we have learned

- When children are taught as a whole group, it is difficult to observe individual differences. What stands out is the children who find what they are asked to do easy to achieve, or possible to achieve. Also noticeable are the children who find the tasks challenging or impossible to do. The children in the middle are not so easy to notice.
- But there can be a group feeling and energy when teaching, an atmosphere during a song sung as a mass crowd, or eating a meal together, or dancing en masse, or experiencing storytelling. The adult leading these events will need to focus on keeping the show going. But this is where the other staff can play an important role by observing in more detail how different children are responding. Teaching as performance and transmission is very different from teaching as an observer who tunes into the detail of a child's response, and is informed by it to know what to do next − observe, support, extend (Bruce, 1987).
- When children have choices about what they do, they show us their strengths. They become more autonomous. Autonomy is about feeling in control (Dweck, 2000) of your learning. It also means knowing what you can manage without help, and knowing how to get help of the right kind, in the right way and at the right time when you don't know what to do, or you reach an impasse in your learning (Matthews, 2003).
- This has important implications for observation which informs planning. The way the room and the garden are set up will have an influence on a child's ability to learn maximally. The presentation of material provision is crucial here. The learning environment needs constant maintaining. Equipment is precious, and cannot be damaged, lost or wasted. Children will help if they are trained to do so and taught to take responsibility for keeping their room attractive to be in. The way that adults work with children is central to the way that children learn. Adults who join children, encourage them to have ideas and 'have a go' will be in a better position to observe each child's learning than those who constantly show children what to do. It is also very enjoyable to work with children in this way. Their creativity never ceases to amaze adults who take the time to engage with them.
- Staff who have themselves experienced use of the materials they provide for the children will have a good understanding of the challenges of a medium. They will be able to recognise as they observe children using the material how far along the learning journey a child is, connecting this to their own learning journeys. This is sharing the learning in the best sense.
- Training is the key to good education. The staff in Soweto are hungry for this, and their work with the Froebel Trust team has led to them being accepted onto courses with UNISA and the University of Johannesburg. One of the staff was asked to give a lesson on shape. She borrowed clay, shape pin boards, slates, sticks and Blu Tack. She asked the children to look around the classroom and identify the shapes, such as square windows or

(Continued)

(Continued)

a rectangular door. They were then invited to make the shapes with the materials she had borrowed. Her tutor was pleased with the practical nature of the mathematics lesson, and commented on how much the children had enjoyed their learning. The staff in this crèche/school have begun to see the value of carefully prepared material provision and the powerful opportunities for teaching of the highest quality that good observation and planning bring.

- It is not easy to create a rich learning environment with virtually no budget and then sustain it without a reliance and dependency on outside help. Pam Mfaxa and her staff have kept going across the years with stamina, commitment, a love of children and a determination for them to have a good education.
- As Nelson Mandela said, 'A movement without a vision is a movement without moral foundation' (1993).

Reflections on this chapter

- Look at the garden and the indoor space where you are working. How sustainable are the materials you use? If carefully looked after, will they last for half a century? Do you have the kind of sustainable materials outlined in this chapter? How many of the observations you make, which inform your planning, are taken in the garden or out of doors?
- How easy would it be to equip your setting with no budget? Would you be able to use non-cost materials and still offer the children a good quality education?
- Do you value training? Do you agree with the message in this chapter, and in this book, that the way practitioners are trained to work with other people's children is an essential part of providing quality of education? What will you do as a result of reading this book to develop your observational skills, so that you will make more and more informed plans to help children in their learning?

Further reading

Bloch, C. (2012) The magic and power of stories and play, *Literacy Issues*, 4 December, pp 1–2.

Bloch, C. (2013) Enabling effective literacy learning in multilingual South African early childhood classrooms, PRAESA Occasional Papers No. 16.

Bruce, T. (ed.) (2012) *Early Childhood Practice: Froebel Today*. London: Sage.

Dowling, M. (2013) *Young Children's Thinking*. London: Sage.

Liebschner, J. (1992) *A Child's Work: Freedom and Guidance in Froebel's Educational Theory and Practice*. Cambridge: Lutterworth.

Whitehead, M. (2010) *Language and Literacy in the Early Years 0–7* (4th edn). London: Sage.

REFLECTIONS

Navigational tools for observation and planning

Observing children, planning for them both in an individual way, and thinking about them as groups with particular needs (e.g. children with English as a second language) require appropriate record-keeping. This allows us to track the progress children make. Records are only useful if they inform practitioners and parents in ways that help them to act on their observations, and so help children to develop and learn.

When records achieve this:

- They keep faith with the heritage and basic principles of the early childhood traditions.
- They help partnership with parents.
- Children are encouraged to reflect on their own learning.
- They are user-friendly and make efficient, effective use of time and energy, so that they are easy to share with parents and colleagues in the team, across disciplines (e.g. the health, social services and voluntary sectors as well as education) and with the child's future teachers.
- They might use a variety of techniques such as written, audio and visual tape recording, photography, files of children's work and records of achievement.
- They link assessment of the child with evaluation of what the child is offered.
- The records inform through sharing, planning and organisation, showing the progress made and next steps.
- They link with current requirements of the day as appropriate, for example the Early Years Foundation Stage.
- They are flexible and grow organically.
- They are capable of a fine focus and they yield specific information.
- They are easy to review and summarise.
- They show starting points, as well as growth points.

Records are about getting to know each child, and what that child needs. Good records give us the navigational tools we require to do this.

BIBLIOGRAPHY

Almy, M. (1975) *The Early Childhood Educator at Work*. New York: McGraw-Hill.

Arnold, C. (1999) *Observing Georgia*. London: Hodder Education.

Arnold, C. (2003) *Observing Harry*. Maidenhead: Open University Press.

Atherton, F. and Nutbrown, C. (2013) *Understanding Schemas and Young Children from Birth to Three*. London: Sage.

Athey, C. (1990) *Extending Thought in Young Children: A Parent–Teacher Partnership*. London: Paul Chapman.

Axeline, V. (1964) *Dibs – In Search of Self*. Boston, MA: Houghton-Mifflin.

Bennett, N. and Kell, J. (1989) *A Good Start? Four Year Olds in Infant Schools*. Oxford: Basil Blackwell.

Bissex, G. (1980) *Gyns at Wrk: A Child Learns to Write and Read*. Cambridge, MA: Harvard University Press.

Bloch, C. (2012) *The Magic and Power of Stories and Play*, Literacy Issues, 4 December, pp 1–2.

Bloch, C. (2013) *Enabling Effective Literacy Learning in Multilingual South African Early Childhood Classrooms*, PRAESA Occasional Papers No. 16.

Bruce, T. (1987) *Early Childhood Education*. London: Hodder and Stoughton.

Bruce, T. (1989) 'Parents as Partners'. Guest Lecture: First International Outstanding Woman Scholar in Education. Virginia Commonwealth University, Richmond, Virginia, USA, *The Link*: 19–23.

Bruce, T. (1991) *Time to Play in Early Childhood Education*. London: Hodder and Stoughton.

Bruce, T. (1997) Adults and children developing play together, *European Early Childhood Education Research Journal*, 5 (1).

Bruce, T. (1999) 'In praise of inspired and inspiring teachers'. In L. Abbott and H. Moylett (eds), *Early Education Transformed*. London: Falmer.

Bruce, T. (ed.) (2004) *Developing Learning in Early Childhood*. London: Sage.

Bruce, T. (2010) Can ABCD help to develop a Froebelian approach to early childhood education in one community in Soweto, South Africa?, *Early Childhood Practice: The Journal for Multi-Professional Partnerships*, 11 (1 and 2).

Bruce, T. (2011a) *Early Childhood Education* (4th edn). London: Hodder Education.

Bruce, T. (2011b) *Learning through Play: Babies, Toddlers and Young Children*. London: Hodder Educaton.

Bruce, T. (2011c) *Cultivating Creativity: Babies, Toddlers and Young Children*. London: Hodder Education.

Bruce, T. (ed.) (2012) *Early Childhood Practice: Froebel Today*. London: Sage.

Butler, D. (1987) *Cushla and her Books*. Harmondsworth: Penguin.

Carr, M. and Lee, W. (2012) *Learning Stories: Constructing Learner Identities in Early Education*. London: Sage.

Carter, C. and Nutbrown, C. (2012) 'The tools of assessment: watching and learning'. In G. Pugh and B. Duffy (eds), *Contemporary Issues in the Early Years*. London: Sage, pp. 127–45.

Chapman, E. (1978) *Visually Handicapped Children and Young People*. London: Routledge and Kegan Paul.

Clay, M. (1985) *The Early Detection of Reading Difficulties*, 3rd edn. London: Heinemann, Primary.

Cooperrider, D.L. and Whitney, D.L. (2001) *Appreciative Inquiry: A Constructive Approach to Organisation, Development and Change*. Cleveland, OH: Lakeshore Publishing.

Corsaro, W. and Molinari, L. (2000) 'Entering and observing in children's worlds: a reflection on a longitudinal ethnography of early education in Italy'. In P. Christennsen and A. James (eds), *Research with Children: Perspectives and Practices*. London: RoutledgeFalmer.

Curriculum for Excellence www.educationscotland.gov.uk

Darwin, C. (1877) 'Biographical sketch of an infant', *Mind*, 2: 285–94.

Davies, M. (2003) *Movement and Dance in Early Childhood*. London: Sage.

Dawes, H.C. (1934) 'An analysis of two hundred quarrels of pre-school children', *Child Development*, 5: 139–57.

Department for Education (2012) *The Statutory Framework for the Early Years Foundation Stage*. London: DfE.

Department for Education (2013) *Early Years Outcomes*. London: DfE.

Department for Education and Employment/Qualifications and Curriculum Authority (2000) *Curriculum Guidance for the Foundation Stage*. London: DfEE.

Department for Education/Department of Health (2011) *Supporting Families in the Foundation Years*. London: DfE.

Department for Education and Skills (DfES) (2002) *Birth to Three Matters: A Framework for Supporting Early Years Practitioners*. London: DfES Sure Start Unit.

Department for Education and Skills (DfES) (2005) *Communicating Matters: The Strands of Communication and Language*. London: DfES.

Department for Education and Skills (DfES) (2007) *Creating the Picture*. London: DfES.

Department of Children and Family Services (DCFS) (2008–10) *Every Child a talker: Guidance for early Years Lead Practitioners*. London: DCFS.

Department of Education and Science (DES) (1974) *A Language for Life* (The Bullock Report). London: HMSO.

Department of Education and Science (DES) (1990) *Starting with Quality: Report of the Committee of Enquiry into the Quality of Education Experience Offered to Three and Four Year Olds. Rumbold Report*. London: HMSO.

Dewey, J. (1963) *Experience and Education*. New York: First Collier Books (Macmillan Publishing Co).

Donaldson, M. (1978) *Children's Minds*. London: Collins/Fontana.

Dowling, M. (2010) *Young Children's Personal, Social and Emotional Development*. London: Sage.

Dowling, M. (2013) *Young Children's Thinking*. London: Sage.

Drummond, M.J. (2008) *Assessment and Values: A Close and Necessary Relationship*. London: Fulton.

Dubiel, J. (2013) 'Tiaras may be optional – the truth isn't: the Early Years Foundation Stage Profile and accurate assessment'. In S. Featherstone (ed.), *Supporting Child-initiated Learning: Like Bees not Butterflies*. London: Featherstone.

Dubiel, J. (2014) *Effective Assessment in the Early Years Foundation Stage*. Huddersfield: Early Excellence Centre for Inspirational Learning and London: Sage.

Dweck, C. (2000) *Self Theories: Their Role in Motivation, Personality and Development*. Hove: Psychology Press.

Early Education (2012) *Development Matters in the Early Years Foundation Stage*. London: Early Education.

Edwards, C., Gandini, L. and Forman, G. (1998) *The Hundred Languages of Children: The Reggio Emilia Approach: Advanced Reflections*. New York: Ablex.

Elfer, P. (2009) *Life at Two: Attachments, Key People and Development*, Siren Films Ltd.

Elfer, P., Goldschmied, E. and Selleck, D. (2012) *Keypersons in the Early Years: Building Relationships for Quality Provision in Early Years Settings and Primary Schools* (2nd edn). London: David Fulton.

Feynman, R. (1981) *Horizon Interview: The Pleasure of Finding Things Out*. BBC TV.

Fisher, J. (2008) *Starting from the Child: Teaching and Learning from 4–8*. Maidenhead: Open University Press.

Forbes, R. (2004) *Beginning to Play*. Maidenhead: Open University Press.

Froebel, F. (1886) *Autobiography of Friedrich Froebel* (translated by E. Michaelis, E. and H. K. Moore). London: Sonneschein.

Froebel, F. (1896) *The Education of Man* (translated by W.N. Hailman). New York: Appleton.

Froebel Trust Project (2013) *Discovered Treasure: The Life and Work of Elinor Golschmied 1910–2009*, DVD and booklet available from www.froebeltrust.org.uk.

Fumoto, H., Robson, S., Greenfield, S. and Hargreaves, D. (2012) *Young Children's Creative Thinking*. London: Sage.

Gibson, J. (1988) *The Psychology of Everyday Things*. New York: Basic Books.

Goldschmied, E. and Selleck, D. (1996) *Communication between Babies in their First Year*. London: National Children's Bureau.

Goldschmied, E., Jackson, S. and Forbes, R. (2014) *People Under Three* (3rd edn). London: Routledge.

Gooch, K. (2010) *Towards Excellence in Early Years Education: Exploring Narratives of Experience*. London: Routledge.

Gopnik, A., Meltzof, A. and Kuhl, P.K. (2001) *How Babies Think*. London: Phoenix.

Grablucker, M. (1988) *There's a Good Girl: Gender Stereotyping in the First 3 Years of Life: A Diary* (translated by W. Philipson). London: Women's Press.

Gura, P. (ed.) (1992) *Exploring Learning: Young Children and Blockplay*. London: Paul Chapman.

Gura, P. (1996) *Resources for Learning: Children, Adults and Stuff*. London: Hodder and Stoughton.

Gussin Paley, V. (1985) *Wally's Stories*. London: Heinemann.

Gussin Paley, V. (2002) *The Kindness of Children*. Chicago: Chicago Press.

Hardyman, C. (1984) *Dream Babies: Child Care from Locke to Spock*. Oxford: Oxford University Press.

Harlen, W. (1982) 'Evaulation and assessment'. In C. Richards (ed.), *New Directions in Primary Education*. London: Falmer.

Harris, D.B. (1963) *Children's Drawings as Measures of Intellectual Maturity: A Revision and Extension of the Goodenough Draw a Man Test*. New York: Harcourt, Brace and World.

Honig, A. (1984) Working in partnership with parents of handicapped infants, *Early Child Development and Care*, 14 (1–2): 13–36.

Hughes, A.M. and Read, V. (2012) *Building Relationships with Parents of Young Children: A Guide to Effective Communication*. London: Routledge.

Hughes, M., Wikeley, F. and Nash, P. (1990) Parents and the national Curriculum. School of Education: University of Exeter.

Hutchin, V. (2013) *Effective Practice in the Early Years Foundation Stage: An Essential Guide*. Maidenhead: Open University Press in association with Nursery World.

Irwin, D.M. and Bushnell, M.M. (1980) *Observational Strategies for Child Study*. St Louis, MO: Holt, Rinehart and Winston.

Isaacs, S. (1930) *Intellectual Growth in Young Children*. New York: Harcourt.

Isaacs, S. (1933) *Social Development in Young Children*. New York: Harcourt.

Isaacs, S. (1968) *The Nursery Years*. London: Routledge and Kegan Paul.

Johnson, H.M. (1933) 'The art of blockbuilding', reprinted in Provenzo, E.F. Jnr. and Brett, A. (1983) *The Complete Block Book*. Syracuse, NY: Syracuse University Press.

Kary, G. (1989) Children's concepts of their own play, in *The Voice of the Child: Conference Proceedings*. London: OMEP.

Katz, L. (1986) *More Talks with Teachers* (chapter 'Assessing the development of pre-schoolers'). Urbana, IL: ERIC/EECE.

Kretzmann, J.P. and McKnight, J.L. (1993) *Building Communities from Inside Out: A Path Towards Finding and Mobilising Community Assets*. Evanston, IL: Institute for Policy Research, Northwestern University.

Laevers, F. and Declercq, B. (eds) (2012) *A Process-Orientated Monitoring System for the Early Years (POMS)*, Leuven: University of Leuven.

Liebschner, J. (1992) *A Child's Work: Freedom and Guidance in Froebel's Educational Theory and Practice*. Cambridge: Lutterworth.

Louis, S. (2012a) The importance of schemas in every child's learning, *Early Education*, Autumn (68): 4–5.

Louis, S. (2012b) Early childhood education in the time of international economic austerity: Is it as easy as ABC (D)?, *Early Education*, International Issue, No. 66.

Louis, S. (2013) From block play to architectural design in a South African kindergarten, *Froebel Trust Newsletter*, www.froebeltrust.org.uk

Louis, S., Beswick, C., Magraw, L. and Hayes, L. (edited by S. Featherstone) (2013) *Understanding Schemas in Young Children, Again! Again!* Available from acblack.com/featherstone

Louis, S. and Miranda, K. (2009) What's their schema?, *Early Education*, Summer (58): 4–5.

Luff, P. (2013) 'Observations: recording and analysis in the Early Years Foundation Stage'. In I. Palaiologou (ed.), *The Early Years Foundation Stage* (2nd edn). London: Sage.

Malloch, S. and Trevarthen, C. (eds) (2009) *Communicative Musicality: Exploring the Basis of Human Companionship*. Oxford: Oxford University Press.

Mandela, N. (1993) Address of Nelson Mandela at his Investiture as Doctor of Laws, Soochow University, Taiwan.

Manning Morton, J. (edited on behalf of colleagues affiliated to London Metropolitan University) (2014) *Exploring Well-being in the Early Years*. Maidenhead: McGraw-Hill/Open University Press.

Marsden, L. and Woodbridge, J. (2005) *Looking Closely at Learning and Teaching … A Journey of Development*. Huddersfield: Early Excellence.

Matthews, J. (2003) *Drawing and Painting: Young Children and Visual Representation* (2nd edn). London: Sage.

Matthews, J. (2011) *Starting from Scratch: The Origin and Development of Expression, Representation and Symbolism in Human and Non-Human Primates*. London: Psychology Press.

Meade, A. and Cubey, P. (2008) *Thinking Children: Learning about Schemas*. Maidenhead: Open University Press.

Moyles, J. (2014) *The Excellence of Play* (4th edn). Maidenhead: Open University Press.

Moylett, H. (ed.) (2014) *The Characteristics of Effective Early Learning: Helping Children to become Learners for Life*. Maidenhead: Open University Press.

Moylett, H. and Stewart, N. (2013) *Emerging, Expected, Exceeding: Understanding the Revised Early Years Foundation Stage Profile*. London: Early Education.

National Children's Bureau (NCB) (2012) *A Know How Guide: The EYFS Progress Check at Age Two*. London: DfE.

Navarra, J.G. (1955) *The Development of Scientific Concepts in a Young Child: A Case Study*. New York: Bureau of Publications, Teacher College, Columbia University.

Nielsen, L. (1984) Letter in *Information Exchange,* October Issue, Royal National Institute for the Blind.

Nielsen, L. (1985) Letter in *Information Exchange,* September No.14, Royal National Institute for the Blind.

Nielsen, L. (1993) *Space and Self: Active Learning by Means of the Little Room*. London: Royal National Institute for the Bline.

Nicholls, R. (ed.) with Sedgewick, J., Duncan, J., Curwin, L. and McDougall, B. (1986) *Rumpus Schema Extra,* Cleveland Teachers in Education, LEA.

Nutbrown, C. (1989a) Up, down and round, *Child Education*, 66 (5): 14–15.

Nutbrown, C. (1989b) Patterns in paintings, patterns in play: young children learning, *Topic 7*, 1. Windsor: NFER.

Nutbrown, C. (2011) *Threads of Thinking: Schemas and Young Children Learning* (4th edn). London: Sage.

Ockelford, A. (2013) *Using Zygonic Theory to Inform Music Education, Therapy and Psychology Research*. Oxford: Oxford University Press.

OFSTED (2013) *Subsidiary Guidance: Supporting the Inspection of Maintained Schools and Academies,* version 3. London: HMSO.

Ollis, J. with Crachnell, L., Nicol, E. and Finke, S. (1990) Parent held development diaries in practice, *Early Years*, 10 (2): 20–7.

Pafford, F. and Savage, L. (2009) Extending thinking in the Early Years Foundation Stage, *Early Education,* Summer (58): 6–7.

Piaget, J. and Inhelder, B. (1969) *The Psychology of the Child*. London: Routledge and Kegan Paul.

Prizart, B.M., Wetherby, A.M., Rubin, E., Laurent, A.C. and Rydell, P.J. (2011) *The Scerts Model: A Comprehensive Educational Approach for Children with AS Disorders, Volume 1, Assessment* (first published 2007). London: Paul Brooks.

Roberts, R. (2006) *Self-esteem and Early Learning: Key People from Birth to School*. London: Sage.

Robertson, J. (1953) *A Two-Year-Old Goes to Hospital* (16mm film, Snd. 45 minutes, English/French). London: Tavistock Clinic.

Russell, A. (2010) *After Mandela: The Battle for the Soul of South Africa*. London: Windmill Books/Random House.

Schenck, R., Nel, H. and Louw, H. (2010) *Introduction to Participatory Community Practice*. Pretoria: University of South Africa Press.

Siren Films *The Two-Year-Old*. www.sirenfilms.co.uk

Siren Films *Physical Development*. www.sirenfilms.co.uk

Stewart, N. (2011) *How Children Learn: The Characteristics of Effective Early Learning,* London: Early Education.

Sure Start (2003) *Birth to Three Matters: A Framework to Support Children in their Earliest Years*. London: Sure Start.

Sylva, K., Malhuish, E., Sammons, P., Siraj-Blatchford, I. and Taggart, B. (2010) *Early Childhood Matters: Evidence from the Effective Pre-School and Primary Education Project (EPPE)*. Abingdon: Routledge.

Sylva, K. and Moore, E. (1984) A survey of under fives record keeping in Great Britain, *Educational Research*, 26(2): 115–20.

Tickell, C. (2011) *The Early Years: Foundations for Life, Health and Learning: An Independent Report on the Early Years Foundation Stage to Her Majesty's Government.* London: DfE.

Vygotsky, L. (1978) *Mind in Society: The Development of Higher Psychological Processes.* Cambridge, MA: Harvard University Press.

Webb, L. (1975) *Making a Start on Child Study.* Oxford: Basil Blackwell.

Weir, R. (1962) *Language in the Crib.* The Hague: Mouton.

Wells, G. (1983) 'Talking with children: the complementary roles of parents and teachers'. In M. Donaldson, R. Grieve and C. Pratt (eds), *Early Childhood Development and Education.* Oxford: Basil Blackwell.

Wells, G. (1987) *The Meaning Makers.* Sevenoaks: Hodder and Stoughton.

West, P. (1972) *Words for a Deaf Daughter.* Harmondsworth: Penguin.

Whitebread, D. (2012) *Developmental Psychology and Early Childhood Education.* London: Sage.

Whitehead, M. (2010) *Language and Literacy in the Early Years 0–7* (4th edn). London: Sage.

Wolfendale, S. (1978) *All About Me.* Psychology Departments: N.E. London Polytechnic.

DVDs

Siren films
Froebel Trust Elinor Goldschmied

INDEX